Teach Yourself VISUALLY™

Sock Knitting

Visual®

by Laura Chau

WILEY

Wiley Publishing, Inc.

Teach Yourself VISUALLY™ Sock Knitting

Published by Wiley Publishing, Inc., Hoboken, New Jersey

For general information on our other products and services or to obtain technical support please contact our Customer Care Department within the U.S. at (800) 762-2974, outside the U.S. at (317) 572-3993 or fax (317) 572-4002.

Wiley also publishes its books in a variety of electronic formats. Some content that appears in print may not be available in electronic books. For more information about Wiley products, please visit our web site at www.wiley.com.

Library of Congress Control Number: 2008932077

ISBN: 978-0-470-27896-3

Printed in the United States of America

10   9   8   7   6

Book production by Wiley Publishing, Inc. Composition Services

Praise for the Teach Yourself VISUALLY Series

I just had to let you and your company know how great I think your books are. I just purchased my third Visual book (my first two are dog-eared now!) and, once again, your product has surpassed my expectations. The expertise, thought, and effort that go into each book are obvious, and I sincerely appreciate your efforts. Keep up the wonderful work!

—*Tracey Moore (Memphis, TN)*

I have several books from the Visual series and have always found them to be valuable resources.

—*Stephen P. Miller (Ballston Spa, NY)*

Thank you for the wonderful books you produce. It wasn't until I was an adult that I discovered how I learn—visually. Although a few publishers out there claim to present the material visually, nothing compares to Visual books. I love the simple layout. Everything is easy to follow. And I understand the material! You really know the way I think and learn. Thanks so much!

—*Stacey Han (Avondale, AZ)*

Like a lot of other people, I understand things best when I see them visually. Your books really make learning easy and life more fun.

—*John T. Frey (Cadillac, MI)*

I am an avid fan of your Visual books. If I need to learn anything, I just buy one of your books and learn the topic in no time. Wonders! I have even trained my friends to give me Visual books as gifts.

—*Illona Bergstrom (Aventura, FL)*

I write to extend my thanks and appreciation for your books. They are clear, easy to follow, and straight to the point. Keep up the good work! I bought several of your books and they are just right! No regrets! I will always buy your books because they are the best.

—*Seward Kollie (Dakar, Senegal)*

Credits

Acquisitions Editor
Pam Mourouzis

Project Editor
Suzanne Snyder

Copy Editor
Carol Pogoni

Technical Editor
Lucinda Lautz

Editorial Manager
Christina Stambaugh

Publisher
Cindy Kitchel

Vice President and Executive Publisher
Kathy Nebenhaus

Interior Design
Kathie Rickard
Elizabeth Brooks

Cover Design
José Almaguer

Photography
Matt Bowen

Photographic Assistant
Andrew Hanson

About the Author

Laura Chau graduated with an H.B.Sc in Biology and Linguistics from the University of Toronto. In spite of this, she spends her time teaching knitting, spinning and dyeing while working at Lettuce Knit in Toronto, Ontario. Laura's handknitting designs for new classic, wearable and fun garments have been featured in Shannon Okey's *Alt Fiber* as well as the online knitting magazine knitty.com.

Laura is the author of the popular knitting blog cosmicpluto knits!, where she discusses her projects and passions, and self-publishes her knitting patterns.

Photo by Michelle Zada.

Acknowledgments

Eternal thanks to my family at Lettuce Knit: Megan Ingman, Denny McMillan, and Alexis DaSilva-Powell. I wouldn't be here without you. The same goes for my family in relation and in heart. A particular debt of gratitude to Stephanie Pearl-McPhee, for opening a door, and to Amy R. Singer for all the opportunities.

Thank you to Linda L. Roghaar, Pam Mourouzis, Suzanne Snyder and Matt Bowen for helping me through the process, and for working so hard to make this book great.

Of course, many, many thanks to my invaluable knitters, who provided their time and needles to produce the many pieces that appear throughout this book: Rachel Arseneau, Jacquie Blackman, Michelle DesGroseilliers, Aleta Fera, Molly Leonard, Kim McBrien, and Stephanie Pearl-McPhee.

Finally, thanks to all my knitterly friends and readers, in person and virtual, for all your creativity, openness, and skill. You inspire me.

Table of Contents

chapter 1 Sock Yarn and Other Materials

chapter 2 Knitting Techniques

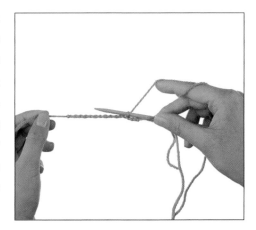

chapter 3 Get Started

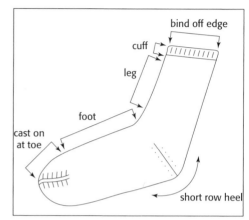

chapter 4 Top-Down Socks

chapter 5 **Flat Socks**

chapter 6 **Toe-Up Socks**

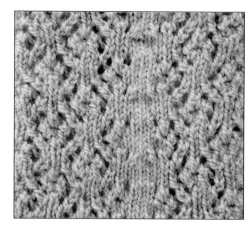

chapter 9 Care for Your Socks

chapter 1

Sock Yarn and Other Materials

When you go to the yarn store and ask for sock yarn, odds are you will face a huge wall full of yarn. Sock yarn is available in an array of colors, fibers, and textures. Nearly any yarn can be used to knit socks, but some yarns work better than others. Different fiber contents and thicknesses will affect the feel, utility, and care of your socks, so carefully consider what you'll make when you pick out your yarn. In this chapter, you learn about different yarn types, fibers, and textures, and how to best use each kind of yarn for socks. Matching a yarn to a pattern is sometimes daunting, so here you also learn how to figure out what yarn works best for different types of sock patterns.

In addition to yarn, you need a few more things to get started. First and foremost, you need needles! Depending on what form of sock you decide to knit, you need either double-pointed, circular, or straight needles. You also need a few important notions. For some types of patterns, you might need some extra tools, too.

Yarn Weights

Yarns are categorized according to thickness into eight main categories. Fingering weight is the most common weight marked as *sock yarn*. Other weights like sport, DK, worsted, and chunky can also make great, fast-knitting socks.

- **Lace Weight:** Lace weight yarns vary greatly in terms of actual yarn thickness. Thicker lace weight yarns can make comfortable, thin socks if knit on an appropriate needle size—US 0 (2mm) or smaller, with a gauge of 10 stitches per inch or more. Two strands of lace weight yarn held together will approximate the thickness of fingering weight yarn (see below). A thick lace weight yarn will measure about 250–325 yards per 50g skein or ball.

- **Fingering Weight:** The term *fingering weight* is often used interchangeably with *sock weight* and is the thickness most often associated with knitting socks. It usually knits up to approximately 7–10 stitches per inch in stockinette stitch on US 00 to US 3 needles (1.75–3.25mm), depending on the thickness of the yarn and how tightly you knit. Fingering weight yarn is sold in amounts ranging from about 180–220 yards per 50g skein. Socks knit from fingering weight yarn are fairly thin and perfect for everyday wear.

- **Sport Weight:** Sport weight yarn is slightly heavier than fingering weight and knits up to approximately 6–7 stitches per inch on US 3 to US 5 (3.25 – 3.75) needles for a dense fabric. Socks made with sport weight yarn are often a bit faster to knit than those made with fingering weight yarn and they feel thicker. Sport weight yarn is sold in amounts of 140–200 yards per 50g skein.

TIP

Check your gauge! Different regions such as the UK or Australia use different terms to label yarn thicknesses. When in doubt about what thickness of yarn you have, just knit a swatch to find out how many stitches per inch you have.

Fingering

Sport

Double knitting

Worsted weight

Bulky

Super bulky

Yarn Weight	Types of Yarn	Gauge Range	Hook in Metric	US Hook Size
1 SUPER FINE	Sock, Fingering	28 – 40 sts	2.0 – 3.25 mm	0 – 3
2 FINE	Sport	24 – 28 sts	3.25 – 3.75mm	3 – 5
3 LIGHT	DK, Light Worsted	20 – 24 sts	3.5 – 4.5 mm	4 – 7
4 MEDIUM	Worsted, Afghan, Aran	17 – 20 sts	3.75 – 5.0 mm	5 – 8
5 BULKY	Chunky	14 – 17 sts	5.0 – 6.0 mm	8 – 10
6 SUPER BULKY	Bulky	8 – 13 sts	6.5 mm and larger	10.5 and larger

Note: This chart reflects the most commonly used gauges and needle or hook sizes for specific yarn categories. These are only guidelines. Used with permission of yarnstandards.com.

- **DK and Worsted Weight:** Double knitting (DK) and worsted weight yarns are similar in thickness, with worsted weight being thicker than DK. Worsted and DK yarns are labeled as knitting to a gauge of 5–6 stitches per inch. However, to create a sturdy, durable fabric for socks, these yarns should be knit at a slightly tighter gauge—approximately 5.5–7 stitches per inch.

  A good rule of thumb is to choose needles two or three sizes smaller than the size suggested on the ball band — rather than a US 7 (4.5mm), try a US 5–7 (3.5–3.75mm) for a good fabric from worsted weight yarn. You need a slightly smaller needle to produce a similar fabric with DK yarn. Worsted weight yarns usually weigh in at 90–100 yards per 50g ball.

- **Aran and Chunky Weight:** Aran weight yarn is sometimes considered *heavy worsted* weight and usually knits up to 4.5 stitches per inch. Aran weight yarn weighs in around 85 yards per 50g skein. To get a good sock fabric with Aran weight, try using a US 5 to US 7 (3.75–4.5mm) needle for a gauge of 5–5.5 stitches per inch.

  Chunky weight yarn is thicker than Aran weight and knits up to 3.5–4 stitches per inch. It comes in skeins or balls of about 60–80 yards per 50g skein. For a dense sock fabric, try US 6 to US 8 (4 –5mm) needles. Aran and chunky weight yarns make thick socks suited for boots or indoor wear.

- **Bulky and Superbulky Weight:** Bulky weight yarn knits up to 3–3.5 stitches per inch, while superbulky weight encompasses any yarn thicker than 3 stitches per inch. Since these yarns are rather thick, they are not the best choice for socks—although they work great for cozy slippers!

Protein Fibers

Protein fibers are derived from animals, and include silk. Wool is the best known of the protein fibers and is used in many sock yarns.

WOOL

Wool is fiber derived from the fur of sheep. It has many excellent qualities which work well for socks. It is breathable, strong, and durable. Wool is also elastic—when stretched, it wants to spring back to its original shape. This fiber is great for knitting socks because they will keep their shape over time.

Different breeds of wool can also wear differently. Fine, soft breeds like Merino are less durable than other breeds and tend to wear out faster. Coarser breeds such as Corriedale or Romney will wear well, but might feel less soft.

Most wool or wool-blend sock yarns are machine washable for easy care. However, always take care to read the label, especially when using a yarn that isn't labeled *sock yarn,* because some yarns require hand-washing.

OTHER PROTEIN FIBERS

Other animal fibers include alpaca, mohair, silk, angora, and cashmere. These fibers can be used to knit socks to great effect. Mohair and silk are quite durable and can take the place of nylon in wool-blend sock yarns. Pure forms of these fibers, however—along with other protein fibers—tend to be less durable than wool and might wear out quickly. Non-wool protein fibers also tend to be much less elastic than wool, which can result in socks that stretch out. These fibers are best used for socks that won't see a lot of day-to-day wear.

BLENDS

Yarns composed of fiber blends can capture the best of all worlds. Wool lends elasticity to inelastic protein fibers as well as plant fibers. Nylon adds strength to all fiber blends. Alpaca and cashmere give a blend of softness and a fuzzier look than pure wool, and silk gives wool a nice sheen.

When considering a blend of wool and synthetic fibers, remember that blends that contain at least 40% wool have the best elasticity and resiliency.

Knit Picks

Traveling the world to bring you affordable knitting

Essential
75% Superwash Wool, 25% Nylon
Meadow Multi

Non-animal fibers are usually made from plants, including the familiar cotton and the less-familiar bamboo, hemp, linen, soy, and corn.

COTTON

Cotton yarns are composed mainly of cellulose. Cotton is breathable, durable, and usually machine washes and dries well. Cotton is also hypoallergenic and is an excellent choice for those with sensitivities to wool or other animal fibers.

However, cotton and many other plant fibers lack the elasticity of wool and can stretch or sag with wear over time. For this reason, many cotton-based sock yarns contain a small amount of elastic (Lycra) to add stretch. Cotton can also be blended with wool to produce a yarn that is cooler to wear than pure wool.

NYLON AND SYNTHETICS

Nylon is a synthetic protein fiber that adds durability to any yarn. Many sock yarns contain some nylon, up to 50% of the fiber content. For socks that will see a lot of wear, choose a yarn containing nylon to extend the life of the socks.

Many synthetics are on the market, mainly acrylic and polyester. These yarns are strong, inexpensive, and machine washable; however, they do not breathe as natural fibers do and can produce uncomfortable feet! If you are avoiding animal fibers, cotton-synthetic blends work well provided they have some elastic content, usually 1–5%.

OTHER FIBERS

Bamboo, soy, corn, chitin, and milk protein are just some of the newest fibers to come on the hand-knitting market. These fibers are considered manmade from natural sources. Chitin and milk protein are not produced from plants. *Chitin* originates in the shells of shrimp and crab, and of course *milk protein* is derived from animal milk. All of these fibers are very durable, but inelastic, like cotton. They carry the same risk of sagging or stretching out over time, so consider blends with elastic or elastic fibers for knitting socks. These cutting-edge fibers are sure to show up in more yarns in the future.

With the vast array of colors and styles of yarn available today, how can you distinguish between the different types? How do you choose the right kind of yarn for your sock project? This section can help.

MACHINE-DYED SOLID YARNS

Most yarns from large companies are dyed in batches by machine to precise shades. Solid light-colored yarns are great for learning with, because the stitches are easy to see. They also lend themselves to showing off complex stitch patterns. Make sure you purchase enough yarn of one dye lot to complete your sock project. A yarn's dye lot (usually a number) can be found on the ball band, and identifies balls of yarn which were dyed together and match exactly. Dye lots can sometimes differ enough to be identified with the naked eye.

When buying yarn for socks, pay close attention to the yardage – one 100 g skein (or 2 50 g skeins) is usually enough for a pair of plain adult socks, but lace socks may use less and cabled or patterned sock a bit more. Check your pattern against your yarn to make sure you have enough!

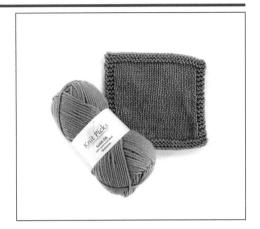

MACHINE-DYED PATTERNING YARNS

Some yarns are dyed precisely by machine to knit up into patterns such as stripes or faux Fair Isle, and are labeled *self-patterning* or *self-striping*. These yarns can be used very effectively to yield a complex-looking sock knit in plain stockinette stitch. A word of warning: The patterns are dyed based on a specific gauge, so if yours differs from that noted on the ball band, the look of the pattern might be different than you expect. Some self-patterning yarns have a photo of a swatch or finished sock printed on the ball band to give you an idea of how it looks knitted up.

HAND-DYED SOLID YARNS

Hand-dyed yarns are usually dyed in smaller batches than machine-dyed yarns and can vary much more from skein to skein. Both solid and multi-colored yarns may be dyed by hand. Hand-dyed solids usually have some shading effects that lend depth to the color and can add interest to a highly textured pattern while still showing off the stitches.

HAND-DYED MULTICOLORED YARNS

Hand-dyed, multicolored sock yarns are all the rage. Multicolored yarns are fun and interesting to knit with, and can produce different effects depending on how the yarn was dyed, as well as the gauge of the piece. Space-dyed or hand-painted yarns in a few colors are more likely to stripe, produce "pools" of certain colors, or produce zigzags of color than behave evenly.

TIP

Yarns dyed with many colors, such as speckles, are more likely to knit up into a random pattern. The more colors that are present in the yarn, the less likely the colors will pool.

Match Your Yarn to Your Pattern

The type of yarn you choose can greatly impact the look of your finished socks. Nearly any yarn will work for a plain stockinette sock, but what about when using a more complex pattern? Let's take a look at how different yarns and colors interact with different types of stitches.

STITCH DEFINITION

Yarn has good stitch definition when the eye can easily distinguish each stitch. Stitch definition is important when choosing yarn for very textured patterns, such as cables—a cable knit in a yarn with good stitch definition will *pop* to the eye more than a cable knit in a yarn with less stitch definition. Yarns with good stitch definition are usually smooth and tightly spun, with little or no *halo* (fuzziness).

DURABILITY

Consider the type of wear your hand-knit socks will get when choosing a yarn—special occasion only? Go for the softest merino wool, maybe blended with some silk or cashmere for extra luxury. Knitting a thick boot sock that will get lots of wear? Choose a more durable, tightly spun non-merino wool for more longevity.

TIP

You can give less durable fibers like cashmere a longer lifespan by knitting the socks tighter than usual on needles a size or two smaller.

COLOR INTERACTION

Although multicolored yarns are beautiful to look at in the skein, complex stitch patterns such as lace or texture patterns can get lost in the mix of colors. It is also more difficult to knit a texture pattern in a highly variegated color, because the stitches are not as easy to see.

Solid or tone-on-tone colors work best for cables, lace, or other textured patterns. Hand-dyed, semisolid yarns are often very attractive in cabled or lace patterns, provided there is not a huge range in the intensity of the color.

Highly variegated colors often look best in stockinette, ribbing, or patterns which incorporate biasing stitches, such as a chevron stitch. Slip-stitch color patterns can help break up random hand-painted colors and prevent the color from pooling or striping.

Needle Materials

Knitting needles come in all types of materials, shapes, and colors, and range greatly in price. You can often find secondhand needles at thrift shops or garage sales. Keep in mind that you'll use your needles over and over again, so take the time to find needles that you really like to use.

BAMBOO

Bamboo is a fast-growing plant that is gaining in popularity as a material for all sorts of things. Because of bamboo's fast growth rate, this crop can be grown sustainably as an alternative to slow-growing trees.

Bamboo needles are strong, flexible, and feel warm in your hands. They can be quite *grippy,* meaning the stitches will not slide as easily as with other materials. This prevents the dreaded *slide-out* where stitches slip off the needles, but is slower for some knitters. With wear, bamboo needles will become more polished and smoother, developing a nice patina.

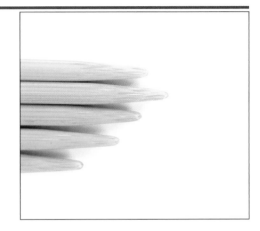

WOOD

Wooden needles, made of materials such as birch and rosewood, are also quite popular. Wooden needles are more expensive than other materials because of the cost of the wood itself. Wooden needles are either mass-produced or handmade. Needles that are hand carved from exotic wood are both beautiful and functional!

Wooden needles are also warm in the hands and flexible, although they are less flexible than bamboo. Generally, wooden needles are more highly polished than bamboo ones and offer more slip in the stitches.

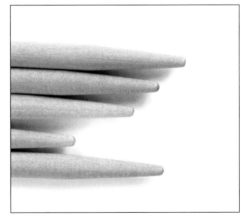

TIP

If your wood or bamboo needles develop a splinter or burr at the tip, you can sand it lightly using a nail file. You can also seal the area with clear nail polish.

PLASTIC

The most widely available needle material, plastic is lightweight and inexpensive. Depending on the style, plastic needles can range from quite slick to very grippy, like bamboo. They can be very flexible, rigid like metal, or somewhere in between. Plastic needles are available in a wide variety of colors and styles.

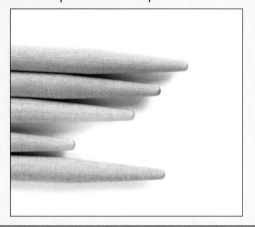

METAL

Made of steel or aluminum, metal needles are usually inexpensive and stitches slide easily on their slippery surface. Be careful with double-pointed needles as stitches can slip completely off the needles when you least expect it! Metal needles are quite rigid and can be uncomfortable if you have hand or wrist ailments.

CASEIN

Needles made from *casein,* a milk protein, feel and look like plastic needles. They tend to be extremely flexible, even more so than most bamboo or plastic needles, and are available in a variety of finishes, from different colors to textures like faux tortoise shell. Some say that casein needles are especially tantalizing to household pets, so keep them away from the dog!

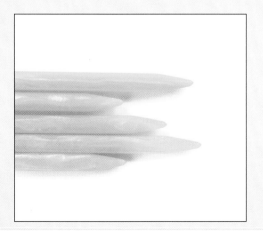

OTHER MATERIALS

Knitting needles are now made of lots of other types of materials, including sterling silver and glass (don't drop them!). Many of these needles are handmade, artisan pieces with prices to match.

You might find vintage needles made of bone or Bakelite, which are collector's items for many. Keep an eye out at garage sales or auctions for these extra-special heirloom needles.

Needle Types

Knitting needles come in several different styles. What most people think of as knitting needles are straight needles, but circular and double-pointed needles are just as common. The type of needles you will need depends on what style of sock you are knitting—and your preference for knitting in the round (round/round); or flat (back/forward).

DOUBLE-POINTED

Double-pointed needles are generally small, 5–7 inches in length. They come in packages of four or five. Sets of five are preferable, even if you like working with four needles—if one needle breaks, you still have enough to work with.

Short double-pointed needles are perfect for smaller projects or if you have trouble holding longer needles. Longer double-pointed needles are preferable for larger projects so that the stitches on each needle have room to move without danger of falling off the ends of the needles.

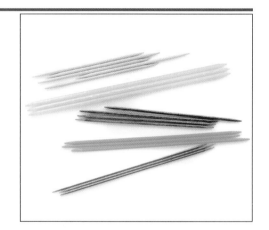

CIRCULAR

Circular needles are composed of two solid tips connected by a flexible cord. They come in various lengths, the most common being 16", 24", 32", and 40". A smooth join between the needle and cord is important for ease of use, as is a flexible cable.

For the two-circular method of sock knitting (see p. 48), you need two circular needles of the same size. Length can differ between the two, but generally shorter needles of 16" or 24" are used.

For the one-circular magic loop method of knitting in the round (see p. XX), you need one circular needle of at least 32" in length. A 40" needle is ideal for learning, but can be cumbersome once you are comfortable with the method.

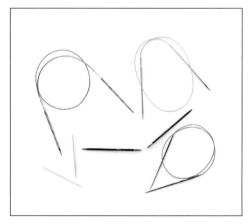

STRAIGHT

Straight needles come in all sorts of lengths, ranging from 9" to 14" long and beyond. Choose a length of needle that accommodates all stitches comfortably and enables you to knit comfortably. Some people tuck the end of the needle under an arm for anchoring; for this, the longest needles you can find are useful. For knitting in cramped spaces, shorter needles are perfect. When knitting socks flat rather than in the round, either straight needles or circulars can be used.

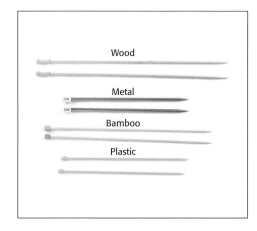

Wood

Metal

Bamboo

Plastic

CHOOSING NEEDLE SIZES

Choosing the right needle size to use with the yarn you select is important. A too-large needle produces a loose fabric, which will not wear well in socks. A too-small needle is difficult to work with, because the fabric is so dense.

The needle size you choose depends quite heavily on how you knit—if you tend to knit tightly, you might need a larger needle size than someone who knits loosely when using the same yarn.

As a general rule, most yarns labeled *sock yarn* suggest an appropriate needle size to use to produce a good fabric for socks.

However, when using thicker yarn such as DK or worsted weight, you should go 2–3 needle sizes down from the suggested needle in order to get a dense fabric.

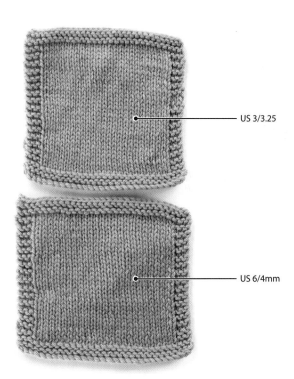

US 3/3.25

US 6/4mm

You will need a few basic notions when getting started knitting socks. Many are not necessary for all patterns, but are often useful when dealing with a more complex pattern.

TAPESTRY NEEDLE

A tapestry or darning needle is usually made of either metal or plastic, with an oversized eye to accommodate yarn. They might come in packages of two or more, either straight or bent tips, and various diameters and lengths.

For socks, you will need a tapestry needle for grafting (see pages 78–80) the toe on top-down socks and for weaving in the ends on all socks. Choose a needle size that fits comfortably through your stitches.

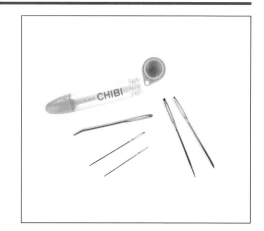

ROW COUNTERS

Clicking the top of the *click counter* (a) advances the number. This counter is quite large and is not attached to the work.

The traditional row counter slips onto the end of a straight knitting needle where the stopper holds it. On double-pointed needles, thread scrap yarn or a large pin (such as a kilt pin) through the counter, then through the sock work. The counter hangs off the work (b). You can also keep the counter separate and just turn the dial after each row.

a

b

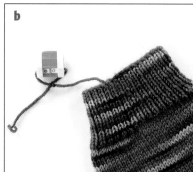

TAPE MEASURE

You can use either a soft tape measure (dressmaker's tape measure) or a hard ruler to measure lengths as you knit. A soft tape measure is essential for measuring around parts of the foot to ensure a proper-fitting sock!

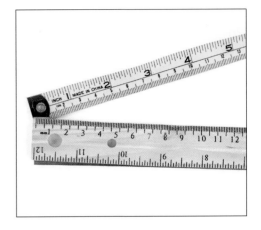

CROCHET HOOK

Although not strictly a notion, a crochet hook is invaluable in sock knitting. You'll need it for a crochet provisional cast-on if you're knitting a toe-up sock. A crochet hook is also very useful for fixing dropped or incorrect stitches as well as for picking up stitches along the edges of heel flaps.

Choose a crochet hook of a comparable size to your needles—a US B or C (2.25mm, 2.75mm) hook for 2.0 – 2.75mm needles and so on. Smaller steel crochet hooks, such as sizes 3 and 4, can also come in handy when knitting with fine yarns.

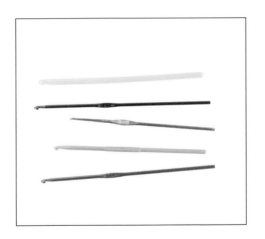

STITCH MARKERS

Stitch markers are closed or locking rings that either sit on the needle or are clasped into the work. They indicate the beginning of the round or other important places in the work, such as where a decrease will occur.

Choose a size of marker that is close to, but larger than the needles you are using.

To use a closed stitch marker, place it on the right needle and continue knitting across your row or round. When you come to the marker on the next row or round, slip it from the left needle to the right and continue.

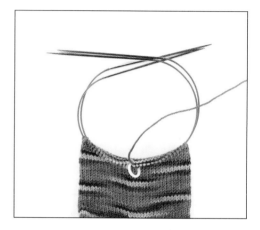

To use a locking or split-stitch marker in the work, place the marker through a stitch or between stitches below the row currently on the needles. You might need to move this marker up the work as you progress.

NEEDLE/GAUGE CHECK

A needle or gauge check is usually a flat piece of metal with holes ranging in size from small to large, a cut-out section (sometimes L-shaped), and ruled edges. To double-check the size of your needles, especially if they are not labeled, place one of the needles through a hole of similar size. Try different-sized holes until the needle just fits through; this is your needle's size.

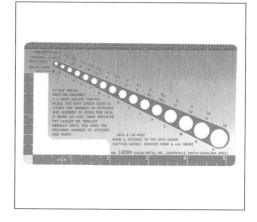

PENCIL AND PAPER

A pencil and paper are handy for keeping track of rows that have multiple patterns, or for taking notes on your work so that you can duplicate it (such as for the second sock!).

TIP

MAGNETIC BOARD

A magnetic board consists of a backing piece and a magnetic strip. A piece of paper, such as a pattern, is placed against the backing piece and held there by the magnetic strip. This tool is especially useful when knitting from a chart or developing a pattern.

To keep track of rows you can place the magnetic strip under or over the row of the chart on which you are working.

chapter 2

Knitting Techniques

You should know several knitting techniques before starting your first socks—cast on, knit, purl, and bind off. Once you are familiar with these skills, incorporating shaping is easy. Socks make a great learning project for picking up stitches, increasing, decreasing, short rows (pages 68–69), and grafting (pages 78–80).

Once you master simple rectangular shapes in your knitting, you're ready to incorporate shaping. Increases and decreases shape the knitting by changing the number of stitches. These stitches are also used in many stitch patterns to create interesting fabrics. Shaping stitches are used in socks to create the curves for the heel and toe, resulting in a sock that will fit your foot exactly.

Cast On

The cast-on is the very beginning of any sock. Here is one common method of casting on for top-down or flat socks, but you can use any cast-on you like such as the Cable Cast-On or Knitted Cast-On. Toe-up socks have their own methods, described in Chapter 9. The main concern in the cast-on is getting the right amount of tension—the sock should stay up, but not be binding.

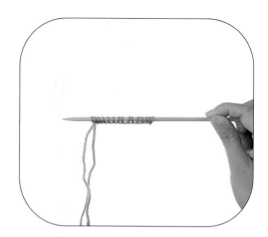

Long-Tail Cast-On

The long-tail cast-on is an easy method that results in a firm yet stretchy edge, and uses only one of your needles. This cast-on seems to have a lot of steps, but once you get the hang of it, the long-tail cast-on is fast and even.

1 Begin by pulling a *long tail* from the end of the working yarn–the amount depends on the number of stitches that you need to cast on. A good general rule is 1 inch per stitch in worsted weight or DK yarn, more for bulky yarns, and less for finer yarns. For a sock, about one arm's length should suffice.

2 Make a slipknot using the end of the yarn not attached to the ball as the "short" end, and place the slipknot onto a knitting needle.

3 Hold this needle in your right hand, allowing the two tails to hang straight down. Place your left index finger and thumb together and place them between the two tails. Grasp the two tails together and drop the left hand below the fingers.

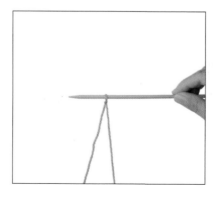

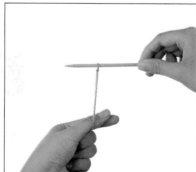

④ Open the index finger and thumb, separating the two strands of yarn. Bring the needle in your right hand down to the level of the left hand, and rotate the left hand so that the index finger and thumb point upward. This is the starting position of the long-tail cast-on.

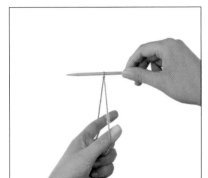
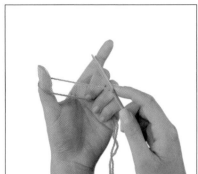

⑤ Bring the right needle tip up under the closest strand of yarn (which loops around the thumb).

⑥ Bring the right needle tip over the farthest strand of yarn (looped around the index finger).

⑦ Bring the right needle tip along with the farthest strand of yarn through the loop created by the thumb.

⑧ Drop the loop off the thumb and onto the right needle. One stitch has been cast on. Tighten this stitch on the right needle and return to the starting position.

⑨ Repeat steps 5–8 until you have cast on the total number of stitches.

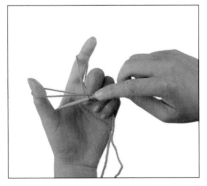

Provisional Cast-On

A *provisional cast-on* is a temporary way to start your knitting—later, you take it out to expose live stitches—and is used in many toe-up socks. You'll need some smooth waste yarn in a similar weight to the working yarn.

One easy method of provisional cast-on is to simply cast on normally with waste yarn, then continue knitting with the working yarn. To expose the live stitches, snip or pull out the waste yarn.

A crochet provisional cast-on, shown here, is easier to undo to expose the live stitches. You need a crochet hook appropriate for your waste yarn and approximately the same size as your knitting needles.

① Make a slipknot out of the waste yarn and place it on the crochet hook. Pull to snug up the slipknot.

② Holding the yarn in your left hand and the hook in your right, bring the yarn over the hook to the left of the slipknot. Use the hook to pull the yarn through the slipknot on the hook, producing a new stitch.

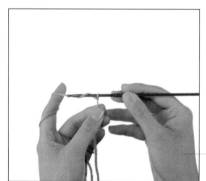
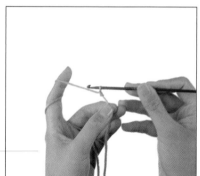

③ Repeat Step 2 until the chain is several stitches longer than the number of stitches you need to cast on.

④ Cut the working yarn and pass the cut end through the last chain stitch. Tie another knot into this tail, so you know which end to pull out later.

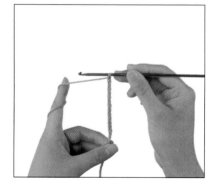
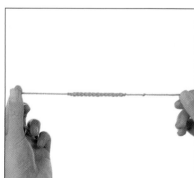

5 The chain is made up of smooth V stitches on one side and bumps on the other side. Lay the chain flat with the bumps facing up. Working from right to left, insert a needle tip under a purl bump.

6 Wrap the working yarn around the needle as if to knit, and pull this stitch through the bump—1 stitch provisionally cast-on.

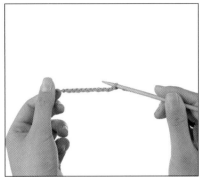 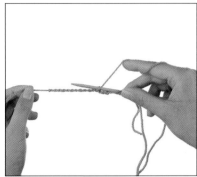

7 Insert the needle tip under the next bump and wrap the yarn around the needle, pulling through the new stitch.

8 Repeat Step 7 until all cast-on stitches are picked up.

9 To remove the crochet chain, locate the end of the chain with the knot. Undo the last stitch of the chain and carefully pull out the chain, placing each live stitch onto a needle as you expose it.

Note: When you place the new live stitches back on the needle, make sure the stitches are oriented properly to knit the next row. See "Twisted Stitch" (page 190).

 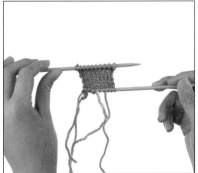

Pick Up Stitches

Picking up stitches from the edge of an already-knit section establishes live stitches and allows you to keep knitting—in the same direction or a different one! In a sock, stitches are picked up along the sides of the heel flap when working a gusset heel.

Pick Up Along Rows

1 Arrange the work with the right side facing you. A set of stitches forms a chain of V shapes along the edge.

2 Starting on the right edge, insert a knitting needle tip under both legs of one V.

3 Wrap the working yarn around the needle counterclockwise as if to knit, leaving a tail several inches long.

4 Use the needle tip to draw the wrapped yarn through the work. This stitch will remain on the needle—1 stitch picked up.

5 Continue onto the next V, inserting the needle under both legs of the stitch, wrapping the yarn, and pulling the new stitch through to the front.

6 When picking up stitches along a heel flap, pick up 1 stitch for each V along the edge. (The edge stitches for a heel flap are slipped as the heel is worked.)

7 When picking up stitches along a non-slipped edge, you need to skip rows occasionally to keep the knitting flat. Pick up 3 stitches one after the other, then skip 1 stitch and continue.

TIP

To pick up stitches evenly, place a locking ring marker through the edge at the halfway point (or quarters if there are lots of stitches to pick up). When you reach the halfway point, you should have picked up half of the stitches required.

Pick Up Along Stitches

1 Arrange the work with the right side facing you and columns of stitches running vertically. Each stitch is one V.

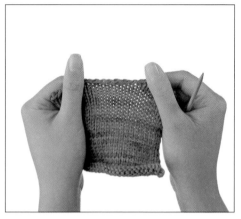

2 Starting at the right edge, insert a knitting needle tip into the middle of the first V.

3 Wrap the working yarn around the needle counterclockwise as if to knit, leaving a tail several inches long.

4 Use the needle tip to draw the wrapped yarn through the work. This stitch will remain on the needle—1 stitch picked up.

⑤ Continue onto the next V, inserting the needle into the center of the stitch, wrapping the yarn, and pulling the new stitch through to the front.

⑥ Pick up 1 stitch in each existing stitch.

TIP

Make sure you are picking up each stitch at the same depth as the previous one. You should be inserting your needle into the stitches of one row across.

Increase: Knit Front and Back, Purl Front and Back

Knit into the front and back of a stitch, abbreviated kf&b, is also referred to as a bar increase and employs a stitch from the previous row. The purl version of this increase is abbreviated pf&b.

Knit into the Front and Back of a Stitch

1 Knit the stitch normally, but do not remove the completed stitch from the left needle.

2 Swing the right needle tip around to the back of the left needle and insert the right needle tip into the back of the stitch from right to left.

3 Wrap the working yarn around the right needle tip counterclockwise and pull the new stitch through the existing stitch.

4 Pull the completed stitch from the left needle to complete the increase—2 knit stitches have been created out of 1 stitch.

Purl into the Front and Back of a Stitch

1 Purl the stitch as normal, but do not remove the completed stitch from the left needle.

2 Swing the right needle tip around so that it is behind the left needle tip. Insert the right needle tip into the back loop of the purl stitch, from left to right.

3 Wrap the working yarn around the right needle tip counterclockwise and pull the new stitch through the existing stitch.

4 Pull the completed stitch from the left needle to complete the increase—2 purl stitches have been created out of 1 stitch.

Increase: Make 1

A Make 1 (M1) increase is also referred to as a *lifted increase*, and uses a stitch from the previous row. This increase can lean either to the right or the left.

Make 1 Knitwise

1 Pick up the bar between 2 stitches from front to back, using the left needle tip.

2 Knit into the back of this stitch, which twists it, to complete the increase. This is a left-leaning increase.

3 To produce a right-leaning increase, pick up the bar between the needles from back to front. Knit into the front of the stitch to complete the increase.

Note: Left- and right-leaning M1s are mirror images of each other and are used on opposite sides of shaping. When no direction is specified, you can use all left-leaning M1s.

Make 1 Purlwise

1 With the yarn in front, pick up the bar between the stitches from front to back, using the left needle tip.

2 Purl through the back loop to complete the increase. This is a left-leaning increase.

3 For a right-leaning increase, pick up the bar between the needles from back to front. Purl into the front of the stitch to complete the increase.

TIP

Twisting the stitch prevents holes from forming where the bar is picked up. If you get a hole, check to make sure you are twisting the stitch as you knit it by knitting into it from the opposite direction from how you picked it up.

Decrease: Knit 2 Together, Purl 2 Together

Knit 2 together, abbreviated as k2tog, is simple to work and decreases by 1 stitch. It is a right-leaning decrease. The purl version of this decrease is abbreviated p2tog.

Knit 2 Together (K2Tog)

1 Insert the right needle tip into the next 2 stitches on the left needle, working from left to right.

2 Wrap the working yarn around the right needle tip counterclockwise.

3 Pull the new stitch through the 2 existing stitches on the left needle.

4 Remove the 2 completed stitches from the left needle. You have knit 2 stitches together into 1, and decreased by 1 stitch.

Purl 2 Together (P2Tog)

1 With working yarn in front, insert the right needle tip into the next 2 stitches on the left needle, from right to left.

2 Wrap the working yarn around the right needle tip counterclockwise.

3 Pull the new stitch through the 2 existing stitches on the left needle.

4 Remove the 2 old stitches from the left needle. You have purled 2 stitches into 1, and decreased by 1 stitch.

Decrease: Slip, Slip, Knit

Slip, slip, knit, abbreviated as ssk, is a left-leaning decrease and is often used as a mirror image to a k2tog. Use this technique to decrease by 1 stitch.

1 Slip 1 stitch from the left needle to the right as if to knit—this twists the stitch.

2 Slip one more stitch from the left needle to the right knitwise. Two slipped stitches are now seated on the right needle.

3 Insert the tip of the left needle into the *front* of these 2 stitches from left to right.

4 Wrap the working yarn around the right needle tip counterclockwise.

5 Pull the new stitch through the existing 2 stitches from back to front.

6 Remove the 2 existing stitches from the left needle. You just knit 2 stitches together to decrease by 1 stitch.

Slip 1, knit 1, pass slipped stitch over is often abbreviated skp. This left-leaning decrease is used as a mirror image to a k2tog. An skp can be interchanged with an ssk, but looks slightly different.

① Slip 1 stitch from the left needle to the right knitwise.

② Knit the next stitch on the left needle.

③ Using the left needle tip, pull the slipped stitch (the second stitch from the tip on the right needle) up and over the knit stitch and off the needle.

Knit Cables

Cables result from crossing groups of stitches over each other; therefore, you knit them out of the usual order. They range from simple ropes or braids to large, complex motifs with multiple crosses and twists.

Cable needles are short needles that come in many different types—straight, curved, or U-shaped—and sizes—wood, plastic, or metal. Choose a cable needle that is the same diameter as your knitting needles.

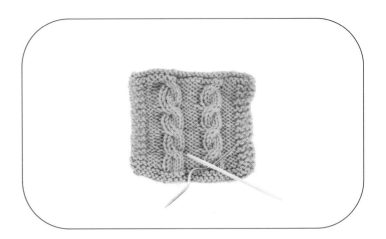

Work a Left-Leaning Cable (C4B)

C4B is the abbreviation for a left-leaning cable, which is worked over a total of 4 stitches.

1 Work to the point of the cable. Slip the next 2 stitches purlwise, but with the yarn in back, to a cable needle.

2 Hold the cable needle behind the main work (and main needles); this represents the *B* (for *behind*) in C4B.

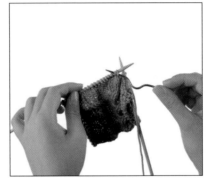

3 Knit the next 2 stitches on the left needle.

4 Knit the 2 slipped stitches that are on the cable needle. Depending on the type of cable needle, you might find it easier to slip these stitches back to the left needle before knitting them.

Work a Right-Leaning Cable (C4F)

C4F is an abbreviation for a right-leaning cable, which is worked over a total of 4 stitches.

1. Work to the point of the cable. Slip the next 2 stitches purlwise, but with the yarn in back, to a cable needle.

2. Hold the cable needle in front of the main work and needles.

3. Knit the next 2 stitches on the left needle.

4. Knit the 2 slipped stitches that are on the cable needle. Depending on the type of cable needle, you might find it easier to slip these stitches back to the left needle before knitting them.

FAQ

What about other kinds of cables?
Cables come in different types and orientations. Whenever a pattern uses a cable abbreviation, a key or listing in the pattern notes explains how to perform the cable.

Weave in Ends

Once your knitting is done, you need to weave in the ends. Socks don't generate a lot of ends, unless you are working stripes or other color work, or you have very small balls of yarn!

Weave in Ends

1. Bring the tails of the yarn to the inside of the sock and thread the end of the tail onto a tapestry needle.

2. Weave in the end with duplicate stitch (see Duplicate Stitch, pages 201–202), using the tapestry needle to guide the yarn tail along a path made by an existing stitch.

3. When working a more complex stitch pattern, weaving in ends with the duplicate stitch method is sometimes difficult. Take your cue from how the wrong side of the fabric looks in order to decide how to weave in your ends.

4. Weave the yarn into the fabric along a row in one direction, then back along the next row. You can also weave in along a stitch column, moving up the column and then down the next.

5. Weave the yarn in for at least 1–2 inches. Cut the yarn, leaving a ½-inch tail.

Blocking refers to a process of finishing that makes your work look extra polished. Blocking smooths out irregularities and makes the fabric more cohesive. It is also useful to make lace patterns stand out. Two main methods are typically used to block socks.

WET BLOCK

1 Wash the socks, either by hand with wool wash or in the washing machine if the yarn allows (check the label). Squeeze or spin out the excess water from the socks without wringing. Roll the socks in a drag towel to remove extra moisture. You can also wet block by spraying the item with water rather than submerging it.

2 Lay the socks flat on a toweled surface and smooth with your hands until the sock is the correct size and shape. Leave to air dry.

Note: You can dry the socks over wooden or metal "sock blockers," which are forms shaped like socks!

STEAM BLOCK

1 Fill your iron with water and set the dial to a steam setting.

2 Once the iron is ready, steam your socks, without touching the fabric to the iron, pulling and shaping the sock with your hands as you go. Again, be sure the iron is only hovering above the sock, not pressing the sock. Be careful, the steam is hot! Allow your socks to cool.

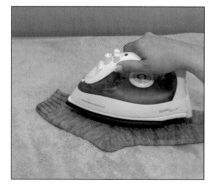

Read Charts

Many stitch patterns are presented through the use of charts. A *chart* is a pictorial representation of the knitted work viewed from the right (public) side. Each box in the chart represents 1 stitch in the knitting.

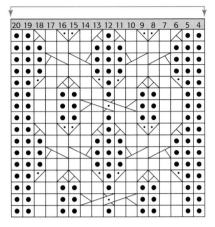

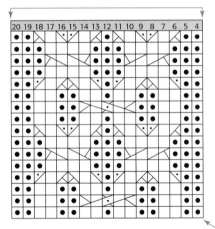

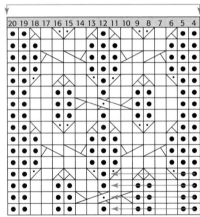

Begin here

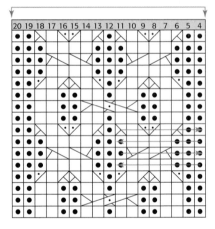

1 The chart begins in the bottom right-hand corner.

2 Read the line in the chart from right to left, repeating the entire box or an outlined portion as necessary, until you get to the end of the line. This is the end of the row.

3 When *knitting in the round,* all rounds are read from right to left.

4 When *knitting flat,* wrong-side rows are read from left to right—so the direction of reading the chart alternates between right to left and left to right on each row.

Read Chart Repeats

Sometimes a chart incorporates stitches that must be worked only once, no matter how many repeats of the main pattern are worked. These stitches occur at the beginning or end of the chart and the beginning or end of the round or row. The main pattern stitches that are repeated are often outlined in red, bolded boxes.

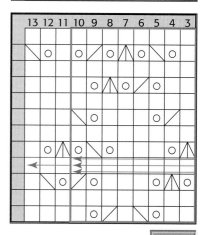

To read this chart, which incorporates non-repeated stitches at the beginning of the round, read the first row all the way across from right to left. Then for the remainder of the round, disregard the black-outlined stitches and repeat only those stitches outlined in red, reading each line from right to left.

To read this chart, which incorporates non-repeated stitches at the end of the round, repeat only those stitches outlined in red until you get to the last stitch, which is the non-repeated stitch outlined in black.

Get Started

Now that you have all the materials you need, you can start on those socks. Nearly all the socks in this book are knit in the round. This technique creates a seamless tube—just like a sock! You can use a variety of methods to knit in the round, and all of them will produce a similar result. Each technique—double-pointed needles, two circulars, and one long circular—has its enthusiastic followers.

To get started on your socks, you first you need to determine the size you need and then make a swatch. Swatching helps you determine if your yarn and needle size are appropriate for your pattern and helps you achieve the correct size.

Using Double-Pointed Needles

Double-pointed needles are usually short (5–7 inches long) with points on both ends. They come in sets of four or five. This lesson demonstrates using a set of five needles.

Cast On with Double-Pointed Needles

1 Cast on all the stitches required for the pattern onto one double-pointed needle.

> **Note:** If the stitches won't fit on one needle, then cast on as many stitches as possible onto one needle and then continue casting on over a second needle.

2 Divide the stitches evenly over four needles by slipping the stitches purlwise one at a time. If the number of stitches isn't divisible by four, simply approximate.

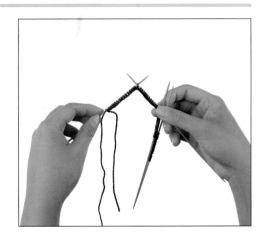

3 Arrange the needles into a square shape, with the cast-on edge to the inside of the needles. You can lay the needles down on a flat surface to check for a twist.

> **Note:** Be careful that the cast-on isn't twisted around the needles or your work will be twisted!

Knit with Double-Pointed Needles

1 Join the first and last cast-on stitches using one of the methods from pages 52–54.

2 To knit in the round, use the empty double-pointed needle to knit across the stitches of the needle to the *left* of where the yarn is joined. Once all the stitches have been worked on this needle, you will again have one empty needle.

Note: The tail from your cast on marks the beginning of the round.

3 Rotate the square of needles to the right and use the empty needle to knit the stitches from the next needle. Pull the yarn tight when switching between the needles to prevent gaps or "laddering" (see pages 192–193).

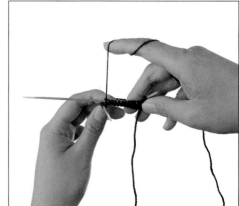

4 Continue to rotate the work and use the empty needle to knit the next set of stitches, all the way around.

The right side of the work (the smooth side with V-shaped stitches when knitting in the round) should appear on the outside of the tube, below the needles.

Note: If the right side is inside your tube, see "Knitting Inside-Out" (page 191).

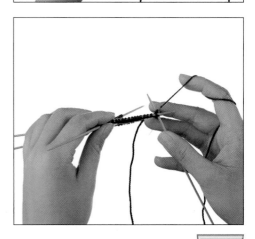

Using Two Circular Needles

Knitting in the round with two circular needles employs two sets of needles of the same size, usually either 16 or 24 inches in length. Using two needles of the same size but different lengths can help you remember which needle is which.

The needles you choose should have flexible cables as well as a smooth join between the needle to the cable. The two circular technique results in only two "corners," rather than four as with double-pointed needles, which can help combat laddering.

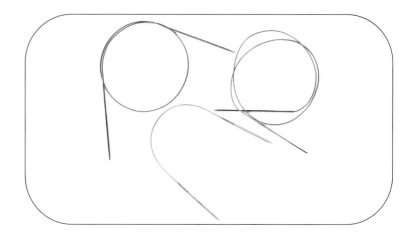

Cast On with Two Circular Needles

① Cast on all the stitches required for the pattern onto one circular needle.

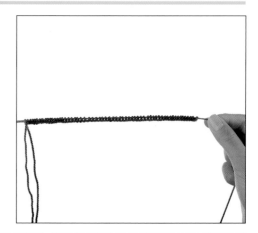

② Place half the stitches onto a second circular needle by slipping them purlwise.

③ Arrange the needles so they are parallel to each other with the cast-on stitches joined at the left edge and the working yarn at the right edge.

④ Join the first and last cast-on stitch using one of the joins found on pages 52–55

Knit with Two Circular Needles

1 Each needle will always work the same half of the stitches. Arrange the needles so that the working yarn is at the right edge and the stitches on the back needle are resting on the needle cord–the back needle (needle B) dangles while you work the front stitches (needle A).

2 Bring the stitches on the front needle up to the needle tip. Using the other end of the same needle, work across these stitches in pattern. The working yarn is now at the left edge.

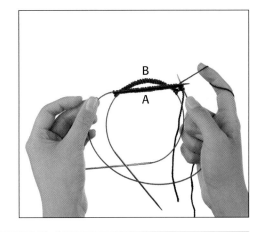

3 Flip the work 180 degrees so that the working yarn is on the right edge. Slide the previously worked stitches (now on the back needle) to the needle cord to rest and bring the stitches on the new front needle up to the tip. Using the other end of the same needle, work across these stitches. One round is now complete.

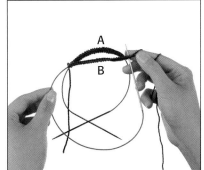

4 Repeat steps 2 and 3 to continue working in the round on two circular needles.

Using One Long Circular Needle (the Magic Loop)

The *magic loop* is a technique that employs one long circular needle to knit small circumferences (such as socks, mittens, or the cuff of a sleeve). You need one circular needle, at least 32 inches (80cm) in length—a length of 40 inches (100cm) is ideal for learning though. As with knitting in the round on two circular needles, make sure that the needle cord is flexible and that the join between the cord and needle tip is smooth.

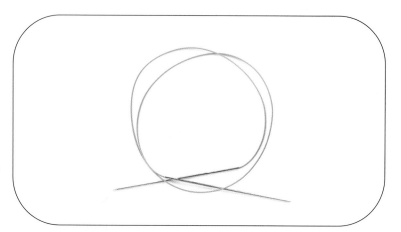

Cast On with the Magic Loop

1 Cast on all the stitches onto a 32- or 40-inch circular needle.

2 Slide all the stitches onto the cable. Count to the halfway point of the stitches and fold the cable in half. Then pull the cord out to create a loop.

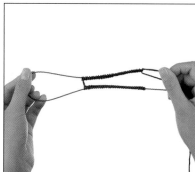

3 Slide the stitches up to the two needle points with the needles held parallel to each other (one in front and one behind) and the tips pointed to the right. The working yarn should come off the first stitch of the back needle.

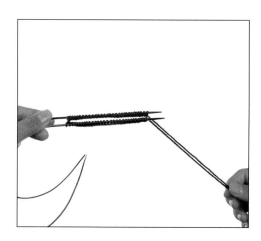

Knit with the Magic Loop

1 Join the round using one of the methods from pages 52–55.

To begin knitting, pull the back needle (furthest from you) to the right so the stitches slide onto the needle cord. Using the now-empty back needle, knit across the front half of the stitches. When you finish this row, the needle holding the completed stitches will be pointing towards the left.

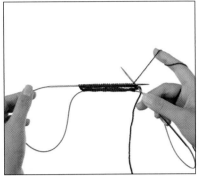 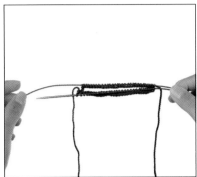

2 Turn your work so that this tip is pointing toward the right again (this will become the new "back" needle). Place the unworked stitches from the cable back onto the empty front needle by pulling the cord or pushing the needle through the stitches. These stitches are now ready to be worked.

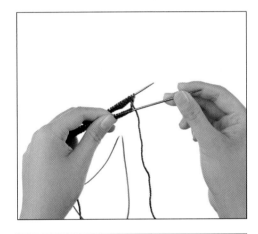

3 Pull the back needle out to the right again, so that the stitches just worked are resting on the cable. Use this needle to work the stitches on the front needle.

4 Repeat steps 1–3 to work in the round with the magic loop.

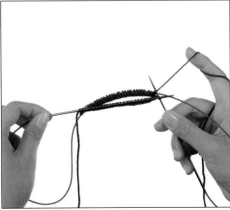

Joins for Knitting in the Round

You can use a couple of different methods for joining your work to knit in the round. Often, a pattern simply states that you should "join without twisting"—it's up to you to decide what method to use. A good join is neat and firm, without leaving a space between the first and last cast-on stitches. Below are several good ways to join.

Simple Join

1 Arrange the needles so that the working yarn is attached to the last cast-on stitch, with this needle on the right.

2 Work into the first stitch of the round (the first cast-on stitch), which is either knit or purl depending on the pattern.

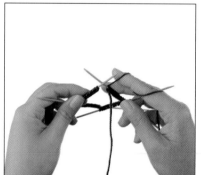

3 When using one or two circular needles, the yarn is attached at the right edge of the back needle. To join, knit the first stitch on the front needle, pulling the working yarn from the back needle.

4 The beginning of the round is between the first and last cast-on stitches.

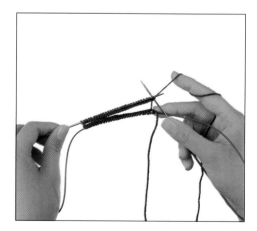

X-Join

1 Arrange the needles so that the working yarn is attached to the last cast-on stitch on the right-hand needle.

2 Slip the first cast-on stitch onto the last needle.

3 Using the left needle tip, pick up the last cast-on stitch, which is now the second stitch from the tip of the right needle. Lift this stitch up and over the first stitch on the needle, keeping it on the left needle tip.

The stitches are now crossed over each other and the join is complete. The beginning of the round is between the two crossed stitches.

CONTINUED ON NEXT PAGE

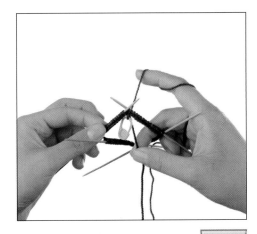

Knit 2 Together Join on Double-Pointed Needles

① Cast on 1 extra stitch than the number required in the pattern. Arrange the needles so that the working yarn is attached to the last cast-on stitch on the right-hand needle.

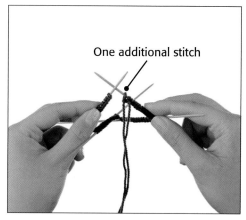

One additional stitch

② Slip the last cast-on stitch onto the left needle tip without twisting.

③ Knit or purl 2 together, depending on the pattern. This is the first stitch of the round.

Knit 2 Together Join on Circular Needles

WHEN WORKING WITH TWO CIRCULAR NEEDLES

1 The extra cast-on stitch is placed on the back needle. Slide both halves of the stitches onto the needle tips, and slip the extra stitch to the front needle, held in your left hand.

2 Place the back (right-hand) needle's stitches back onto the cable.

3 Knit or purl (depending on the pattern) the first 2 stitches together with the front needle. This is the first stitch of the round.

WHEN WORKING WITH ONE CIRCULAR NEEDLE

1 The extra cast-on stitch is also placed on the back needle. Slide all stitches up to the needle tips and slip the extra stitch to the front needle, which is in your left hand.

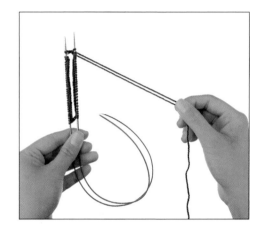

2 Pull out the back (right-hand) needle and knit or purl (depending on the pattern) the first 2 stitches together as the first stitch of the round.

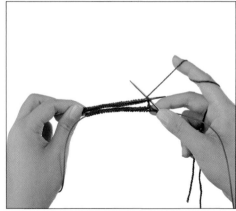

When knitting a project in the round, swatching in the round is important because many knitters get a different gauge when knitting in the round versus knitting flat. Rather than casting on a large number of stitches and knitting in the round for a swatch, you can create the same effect with a faux-round swatch.

1 Cast on 30–40 stitches using the yarn and circular or double-pointed needles of the size you will use for the pattern.

2 Knit 4 rows garter stitch flat, turning the needles as usual when knitting back and forth.

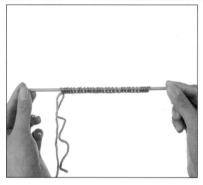 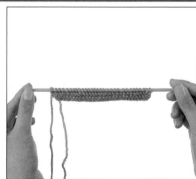

3 Begin working the swatch in stockinette stitch—knit across 1 row. The yarn is now at the left edge of the piece.

4 Slide the stitches to the other end of the needle.

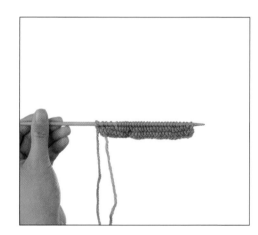

5 Draw the working yarn loosely across the back of the swatch. Knit across the row again.

Continue working even, sliding the piece to the other end of the needle at the end of each row and drawing the yarn loosely across the back. This method simulates knitting in the round because every row is knit from the right side.

6 Work even until the piece measures at least 4 inches. Work 4 more rows of garter stitch, turning after each row as for flat knitting. Bind off.

7 Turn the swatch over and cut through the loose strands of yarn across the back using sharp scissors.

8 Wash the swatch as you would the completed item. Lay flat to dry.

Measure Your Swatch

Measuring your swatch accurately is as important as knitting it correctly! You'll need a ruler or measuring tape and two straight pins or split stitch markers.

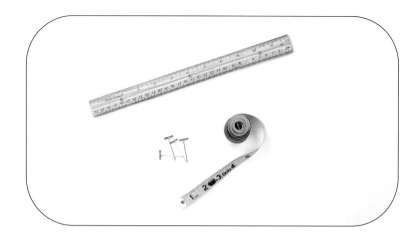

Measure Stitch Gauge

1 Lay your swatch flat on a table without stretching or distorting the fabric. Lay a ruler, needle gauge, or tape measure horizontally on the swatch below a row in the middle of the swatch.

2 Place two pins or split stitch markers in the fabric exactly 4 inches apart.

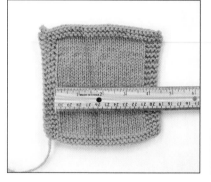

3 Count how many stitches are in 3 or 4 inches, but count only the middle stitches in the swatch (not at the edges). Be sure to count half or quarter stitches, too.

4 Divide this number by the number of inches you measured to get the stitches per inch. For example, if you count 20 stitches in 4 inches, your stitch gauge is 5 stitches per inch.

Measure Row Gauge

1 Lay the swatch flat without stretching the fabric. Lay a ruler, needle gauge, or tape measure vertically on the swatch along one row in the middle of the swatch.

2 Place two pins or split stitch markers exactly 4 inches apart.

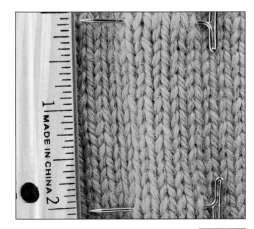

3 Count how many rows are in 3 or 4 inches, including half or quarter stitches.

4 Divide this number by the number of inches you measured to get the rows per inch. If you count 28 rows in 4 inches, your row gauge is 7 rows per inch.

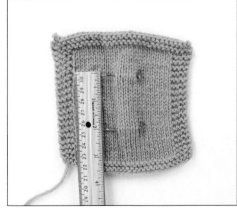

A sock is made up of several different sections with different names. Familiarizing yourself with the various parts will ensure that you always know what you're working on!

The *cuff* is the very top of the sock and the sock is usually either cast on or bound off here. Cuffs are often worked in ribbing to keep the socks up on the leg, or you can work a cuff in a variety of other decorative stitch patterns.

The *leg* is the portion of the sock up to the heel and shows off different stitch or color patterns. The leg is either straight or shaped to accommodate the size of the calf.

The *heel* is a portion of the sock that is shaped to fit around the heel of the foot. You can create a heel in different ways with slightly differing fits—and tube socks have no designated heel at all. Common heel types include the short-row heel and the heel flap and gusset.

The *foot* is the portion of the sock between the heel and the toe. Stitch patterns are most often placed on the top of the foot only, with the sole of the foot worked in stockinette stitch.

The *toe* is the shaped, closed portion at the bottom of the sock. The toe is sometimes shaped differently depending on the shape of the foot and fit preference.

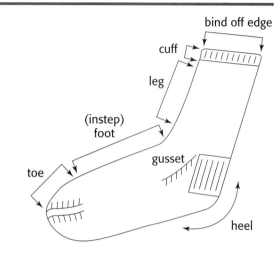

Socks of other constructions might be knit in a different order, but the parts of the sock remain the same. In a *toe-up sock,* the toe is worked first, then the foot, the heel, the leg, and then the cuff. The sock is bound off at the top of the cuff.

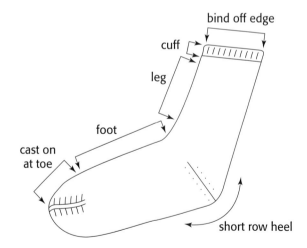

You need to determine a few important foot measurements to figure out what size to knit your socks. For a set of standard approximate foot measurements corresponding to shoe size, see "Sizing Chart and Yarn Requirements" on page 207.

Measure the Ball of the Foot

The *ball* of the foot is the section just below the toes and is the widest section of the foot.

① Wrap a soft measuring tape around the ball of your foot, holding the tape snugly. Read the measuring tape where it overlaps.

② If you don't have a soft measuring tape, use a piece of non-stretchy yarn (such as cotton) and wrap that around your foot, marking where it meets. Lay this against a straight ruler or hard measuring tape to get your foot measurement.

Measure Foot Length

① Stand with your feet flat on the floor. Lay a measuring tape along the inside of your foot (the big toe side).

② Measure from the back of the heel to the tip of your big toe. This is your total foot length.

FAQ

How do I choose which size to make?
For a snug-fitting sock, choose the foot measurement that is one size (usually ½ inch) smaller than your foot measurement. For a looser sock, select the size that corresponds with your measurement.

chapter 4

Top-Down Socks

Socks knit from the top down are what most knitters think of as the traditional method. These socks are easy to cast on and start, with the more involved techniques occurring in the middle and at the end of the sock.

There are many sock patterns written for the top-down method, and within a top-down sock there are many variations of stitch patterns, heel constructions, and toe-shaping methods. This chapter covers some basic types of heels and toes.

Cast On

Any of the cast-on methods described on pages 22–25 will work well for a top-down sock. Just make sure you cast on loosely enough, or your sock will be inflexible at the top edge and might not fit over your foot!

Locate your cast-on number on the chart below by finding your gauge along the left edge and the size needed along the top edge.

Top-Down Socks: Sizes and Cast-On Numbers						
Gauge/Size	Child M	Child L/ W Sm	W Med	W Lrg/ M Sm	M Med	M Lrg
Circumference (in.)	6.5	7.5	8	8.5	9	9.5
5 (US 5-8 needles)	32	36	40	44	48	52
6 (US 4-6 needles)	40	44	48	52	56	60
7 (US 3-5 needles)		52	56	60	64	68
8 (US 1-3 needles)	52	56	60	64	68	72
9 (US 0-2 needles)	60	68	72	76	80	84

After you cast on, join for working in the round and place a marker in the work to indicate the beginning of the round.

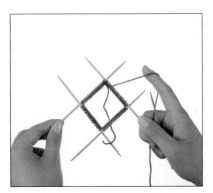
Stitches cast on and joined on double-pointed needles.

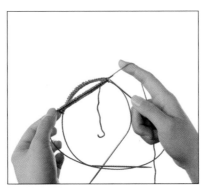
Stitches cast on and joined on two circular needles.

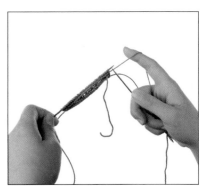
Stitches cast on and joined on one circular needle.

The *cuff* of a sock refers to an edging at the top of the sock of about 1–3 inches (see "Anatomy of a Sock," p. 60). The *leg* of the sock refers to the section below the cuff and above the heel. Of course, you don't have to have a cuff at all. Simply begin your leg pattern right away, but note that some stockinette-based patterns may roll down at the top without an edging.

Continue working straight, in the round, in the stitch pattern of your choice for the cuff and leg.

RIBBING

Ribbing is a classic choice for sock cuffs and legs. Most knitters opt for 1 × 1 or 2 × 2 ribbing.

To work 1 × 1 ribbing, * k1, p1 * and repeat from * to * around the sock.

To work 2 × 2 ribbing, * k2, p2 * and repeat from * to * around the sock.

You can switch from ribbing to stockinette stitch after an inch or two for a cuff, or continue the ribbing straight down the leg for a close-fitting sock.

ADD PATTERNING

The leg is where many sock patterns incorporate different types of stitch patterns, such as cables, lace, or color work. The patterning may then continue down the front of the sock to the toe.

To incorporate a stitch pattern, figure out how many stitches the pattern requires. A lace pattern that has a 4-stitch repeat will fit nicely over any cast-on number from the chart, but it would be difficult to incorporate a 13-stitch repeat.

For more on adding stitch patterns to your basic sock pattern, see Chapter 2.

Knit a Gusset Heel

Once the leg is complete, you will knit the heel. It may look complicated, but only a few simple steps are involved. In order to shape the sock so that it fits around the curve of the foot, the gusset heel consists of three steps—knitting a heel flap, shaping the bottom of the heel, and decreasing for the gusset. The example sock contains 64 cast-on stitches.

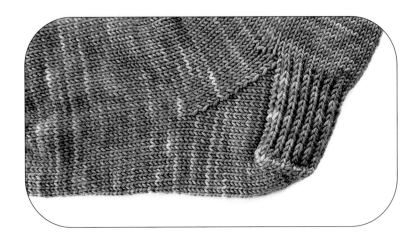

Knit the Heel Flap

The heel flap is typically knit on half the total number of sock stitches and in a slipped-stitch pattern for thickness and durability. You knit it back and forth (not in the round) to produce a *flap* for the back of the heel.

① Knit one needle (25%) of the sock's stitches as follows:

Row 1: * Sl 1 pwise wyib, k1 *, rep from * to * across.

Example sock: Work 16 sts in patt.

② Turn the work so that the inside of the sock is facing you.

3 Work across two needles (50% of the sock's stitches) as follows, working all the stitches onto one needle:

Row 2: Sl 1 pwise wyif, p across.

Example sock: Work 32 sts in patt.

4 Repeat rows 1 and 2 until the heel flap is square—work as many rows as there are stitches in the heel flap.

Example sock: The heel flap is 32 sts wide and 32 rows long.

CONTINUED ON NEXT PAGE

TIP

You can figure out how many rows of heel flap you've knit by counting the large chain stitches on either edge. You'll have half as many chain stitches as the number of heel flap stitches when the flap is done!

Turn the Heel

Turning the heel involves the use of short rows to shape the "cup" at the bottom of the heel. *Short rows* are rows where you only work part of the stitches in the row, leaving some stitches to be worked later.

1 Knit across a prescribed number of stitches—usually a little more than half of the stitches.

Example sock: K 18 sts.

2 Decrease by ssk, then k1. Turn the work to the wrong side.

3 Slip 1 purlwise with the yarn in front, purl 5, p2tog, p1.

Note: Socks with different stitch counts may prescribe a different number of purl stitches on this row.

4 Continue to work short rows as follows:

Row 1 (RS): Slip 1 pwise, knit to 1 st before the gap created in the previous row, ssk, k1, turn.

Row 2 (WS): Slip 1 pwise, purl to 1 st before the gap, p2tog, p1, turn.

5 Repeat these 2 rows until all the stitches of the heel flap are worked, ending with the RS facing for next row. If not enough stitches remain to complete the p2tog, p1 at the end of the last WS row, work as p2tog.

Example sock: 18 sts remain.

CONTINUED ON NEXT PAGE

TIP

For a deeper heel, work more rows in the heel flap before turning the heel. For each 2 additional rows you add to the heel flap, pick up an additional stitch on either side of the heel flap when preparing for the gusset.

Make the Gusset

The *gusset* consists of two parts: picking up stitches to connect the heel flap with the rest of the sock and working decreases to shape the sides of the foot.

1 Knit across all heel stitches (example sock: 18), then pick up stitches with another double-pointed needle as follows:

Insert the tip of the right (empty) needle below both legs of the slipped-stitch column along the edge of the heel flap. Wrap the yarn around the needle as if you were knitting, then pull the new stitch through the work to create a new loop on the right needle.

2 Continue to pick up stitches along the edge of the heel flap, 1 stitch for each slipped stitch along the edge, until 18 stitches are picked up.

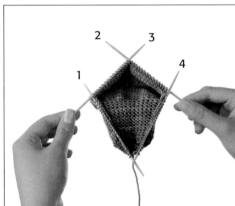

3 Knit across the instep stitches that were held during the knitting of the heel, continuing any pattern if you desire, then pick up 18 more stitches along the other side of the heel flap. Knit across the heel flap stitches—this needle is now called Needle 1 and is the first needle of the round.

TIP

To prevent a hole at the top of the heel flap, you can pick up an extra stitch at the junction between the heel flap and the instep. Continue with the decreases as written until the original number of stitches remain.

4 Work decrease round as follows:

Needle 2: Knit to the last 3 sts, k2tog, k1.

Needle 3: Work across in patt.

Needle 4: K1, ssk, k to end of needle.

5 Knit 1 round even.

6 Repeat the last 2 rows until 64 stitches remain, or the original cast-on number. The gusset is complete! Continue to "Knit the Foot," p. 74.

TIP

To prevent holes from forming at the top of the gusset, pick up an additional stitch at the very corner of the gusset where it meets the instep (top of the foot) on either side of the foot. Continue the decreases as given.

Knit an Afterthought Heel

The Afterthought Heel is added after the entire body of the sock is completed down to the toes. It is easy to replace once worn out; it also lends itself easily to using contrasting yarn for an interesting heel addition.

Knit in Waste Yarn

1 At the end of the leg, knit half of the stitches using a smooth waste yarn of a similar thickness to the working yarn.

Note: Your waste yarn can be a different fiber composition, so long as it's smooth (not sticky) and of an appropriate thickness. You can even use the same yarn as you're knitting with, but make sure it's a different color!

2 Slip these stitches back to the left needle without twisting. Re-knit these stitches in the working yarn and continue working in pattern straight to the toe.

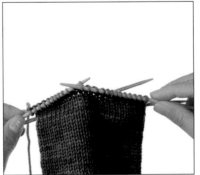

Recover Stitches

Once the toe is complete, you should recover the stitches for the heel.

1 Remove the waste yarn, placing the live stitches onto two double-pointed needles. The heel opening will have the same number of stitches as the sock body.

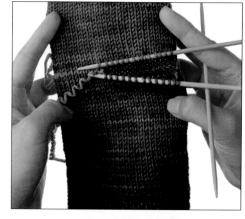

2 Re-arrange the stitches onto four needles, placing markers at each side edge of the heel opening to mark the decrease points.

3 Decrease for the heel exactly as for the Basic Round Toe (see pages 75–76), ending the decreases when approximately 2 inches' worth of stitches remain. Graft together these stitches using the Kitchener Stitch (pages 78–80); this is the bottom corner of the heel.

Once the gusset decreases are complete or waste yarn knit in, you will knit the body of the foot.

For a plain stockinette stitch sock, simply knit every stitch of every round until the foot length measures 2 inches less than the desired total length (approximately at the base of the big toe for adult socks).

If foot measurements are not readily available, refer to the table on page 207 for standard measurements.

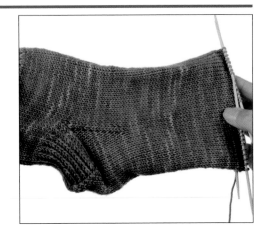

In a patterned sock, you carry the stitch pattern across the top of the foot but work the instep in stockinette stitch. You work the pattern stitch over the two needles holding the stitches of the top of the foot, while working stockinette over the other two needles.

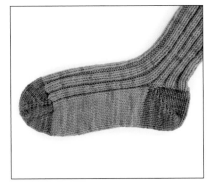

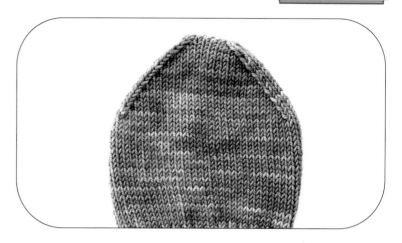

A sock toe is shaped with decreases, with the exception of the short-row toe. Each toe is about 2 inches long, so the leg is worked until 2 inches from the desired length, measured from the back of the heel. The toe is most often worked in stockinette stitch, even if the leg and foot are patterned.

Knit a Basic Round Toe

In the Basic Round Toe, you work decreases on the sides of the sock to the tip of the toe, which is then closed with Kitchener stitch (pages 78–80).

1 The round begins at the middle of the bottom of the sock. Work the toe decreases as follows:

Round 1:

  Needle 1: K to last 3 sts, k2tog, k1.

  Needle 2: K1, ssk, k to end of needle.

  Needle 3: K to last 3 sts, k2tog, k1.

  Needle 4: K1, ssk, k to end of needle.

2 Work Round 2 as follows:

Round 2:

  Knit around on all sts.

CONTINUED ON NEXT PAGE

3 Repeat rounds 1 and 2 until you decrease the total number of stitches to 50%, ending with a Round 2.

4 Repeat Round 1 only until approximately 2 inches' worth of stitches remain—between 10 and 18 stitches depending on gauge.

Continue to close the toe using the Kitchener stitch.

TIP

For a wider toe, decrease fewer times and leave more stitches to graft. For a narrower toe, decrease more times and leave fewer stitches to graft.

In the Star Toe, you work decreases at four points evenly distributed around the sock, producing a swirl or star pattern. The tip of the toe is closed either by grafting (pages 78–80) or gathering (page 81).

Knit a Star Toe

1 The round begins at the middle of the sole of the foot. Work toe decreases as follows:

Round 1:

    Needle 1: K1, ssk, k to end of needle.

    Needle 2: Rep as for Needle 1.

    Needle 3: Rep as for Needle 1.

    Needle 4: Rep as for Needle 1.

2 Work Round 2 as follows:

Round 2:

    Knit around on all sts.

3 Repeat rounds 1 and 2 until you decrease the total number of stitches to 50%, ending with Round 2.

4 Repeat Round 1 only until approximately 2 inches' worth of stitches remain—between 10 and 18 stitches depending on gauge.

Continue to "Close the Toe: Kitchener Stitch" or "Close the Toe: Gather," depending on what your pattern specifies. Grafting will produce a flatter tip of the toe, while gathering will produce a round tip of the toe.

Note: *For a mirror image spiral on the other sock, decrease at the end of each needle rather than the beginning as follows: K to last 3 sts of needle, k2tog, k1.*

Close the Toe: Kitchener Stitch

To close the tip of the toe, you can graft the stitches together using the Kitchener stitch. This creates a seamless closure at the end of the sock.

How to Graft

① Arrange the stitches on the needles so that all the stitches from the top of the foot are on one needle and all the stitches from the bottom of the foot are on another needle, with the working yarn attached at one edge.

② Cut the working yarn, leaving approximately 15 inches of yarn as a tail. Thread the tail onto a darning needle.

③ Hold the sock with the needles parallel so that the working yarn comes off the back needle, on the right edge.

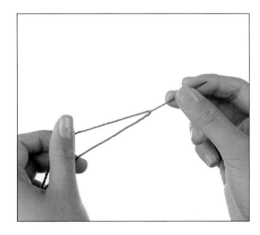

4 Bring the darning needle through the first stitch on the front needle purlwise.

5 Bring the needle through the first stitch on the back needle purlwise, and remove this stitch from the back needle.

6 Bring the needle through the next stitch on the back needle knitwise.

CONTINUED ON NEXT PAGE

⑦ Bring the needle through the first stitch on the front needle knitwise, and remove this stitch from the front needle.

⑧ Repeat steps 4–7 until you work all the stitches.

⑨ Adjust the tension of the grafted stitches by carefully using the darning needle tip to pull up any slack in the stitches, working from right to left across the toe. After you work most of the slack across to the left side of the toe, pull the tail of yarn to tighten.

⑩ Bring the tail to the inside of the sock and weave in the end.

A *gathered* toe is very round and looks like the top of a hat. Closing the toe this way is easy and fast.

Gather the Toe

① Cut working yarn leaving an 8-inch tail. Thread the end of the yarn onto a darning needle.

② Work around the sock, slipping stitches purlwise off each needle onto the darning needle.

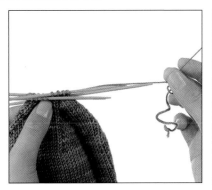

③ Once you have come to the end of the round, thread the darning needle through the stitches again in the same direction.

④ Pull the yarn tight to close the toe and place working yarn to the inside so you can weave it into the sock.

Basic Top-Down Sock Pattern

This basic pattern is for a top-down sock in fingering weight yarn and employs the gusset heel and basic toe.

SIZE

Child M (Child Lrg/W Sm, W Med, W Lrg/M Sm, M Med, M Lrg)

MATERIALS

200 (250, 300, 350, 400, 450) yards of fingering weight yarn

US 1 (2.25mm) double-pointed, two circulars, or one long circular needle, or size to obtain gauge

GAUGE

8 sts and 10 rounds = 4 inches square in St st

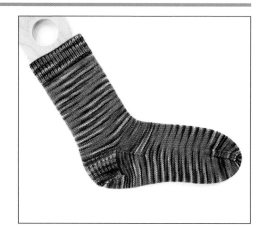

Pattern Stitch

1 × 1 RIBBING

Round 1: * K1, p1 *, rep from * to * around.

Rep round 1 for patt.

Directions for Basic Top-Down Sock (Make 2)

1 Cast on 52 (56, 60, 64, 68, 72) sts using the desired cast-on. Join, being careful not to twist.

2 Work 1 × 1 ribbing until piece measures 1 inch from beg.

3 Continue even in St st until piece measures 5.5 (6, 6.5, 7, 7.5, 8) inches from beg or desired length to top of heel.

WORK THE HEEL

The heel is worked over 26 (28, 30, 32, 34, 36) sts.

1 Next row (RS): K 13 (14, 15, 16, 17, 18) sts, turn.

2 P across 26 (28, 30, 32, 34, 36) sts.

3 Row 1 (RS): * Sl 1, K1*, rep from * to * across.

4 Row 2 (WS): Sl 1, p across.

5 Rep rows 1 and 2 until you have worked 26 (28, 30, 32, 34, 36) rows in total.

TURN THE HEEL

1 Row 1: K across 15 (16, 17, 18, 19, 20) sts, ssk, k1, turn.

2 Row 2: Sl 1, p5, p2tog, p1, turn.

3 Row 3: Sl 1, k to 1 st before gap, ssk (1 st from each side of gap), k1, turn.

4 Row 4: Sl 1, p to 1 st before gap, p2tog (1 st from each side of gap), p1, turn.

5 Rep rows 3 and 4 until you have worked all heel sts, ending if necessary on the last rep with k2tog and p2tog. 16 (16, 18, 18, 20, 20) sts remain.

CONTINUED ON NEXT PAGE

GUSSET

1 Next round: K 8 (8, 9, 9, 10, 10) sts. Using an empty needle, k 8 (8, 9, 9, 10, 10) sts. Rotate work and with the same needle, pick up 13 (14, 15, 16, 17, 18) sts along side of heel flap.

2 Work across 26 (28, 30, 32, 34, 36) sts of instep.

3 Pick up 13 (14, 15, 16, 17, 18) sts along other side of heel flap using an empty needle. K rem 8 (8, 9, 9, 10, 10) sts. The heel is now complete and the round begins at the center back heel.

DECREASE FOR THE GUSSET

Round 1

1 Needle 1: K to last 3 sts, k2tog, k1.

2 Needle 2: Knit all sts.

3 Needle 3: Knit all sts.

4 Needle 4: Ssk, k1, k to end.

Round 2

1 Knit all sts.

2 Rep rounds 1 and 2 until 52 (56, 60, 64, 68, 72) sts remain.

3 Work even on these sts until piece measures 5.5 (6.5, 7.5, 8, 8.5, 9) inches from the back of the heel, or 2 inches less than desired total foot length.

SHAPE THE TOE

Round 1

1 Needle 1: K to last 3 sts, k2tog, k1.

2 Needle 2: k1, Ssk, k to end.

3 Needle 3: K to last 3 sts, k2tog, k1.

4 Needle 4: k1, Ssk, k to end.

Round 2

1 Knit all sts.

2 Rep rounds 1 and 2 until 26 (28, 30, 32, 34, 36) sts rem.

3 Rep round 1 until 12 (12, 16, 16, 18, 18) sts rem.

4 K to the end of Needle 1. Cut yarn and graft toe.

5 Weave in ends and block.

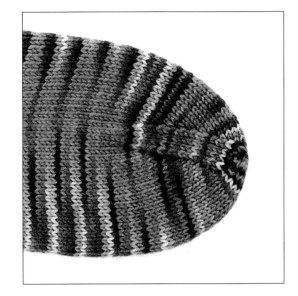

chapter 5

Flat Socks

Although socks knit in the round are practical and easy, you might want to knit a pair of socks flat, on two needles. Some knitters prefer to use straight needles rather than knit in the round, don't own circular or double-pointed needles, or just want to try something different. These basic flat socks have one seam that runs down the back of the leg and two more seams on the foot, one on either side. They are similar in construction to top-down socks knit in the round.

Cast On

Cast on for your flat sock with one of the methods on pages 22–25 using straight needles or knitting back and forth on circular needles.

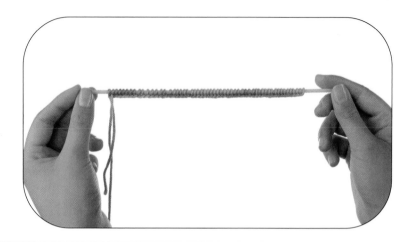

Use the cast-on numbers according to the chart below. It is a modification of the chart for top-down socks found on p. 64. Keep in mind that you will use 2 stitches in the leg and 4 stitches in the foot for seaming. You might want to cast on for a larger size to compensate for these lost stitches.

Gauge/Size	Child M	Child L/W Sm	W Med	W Lrg/M Sm	M Med	M Lrg
Flat Socks: Sizes and Cast-On Numbers						
Circumference (in.)	6.5	7.5	8	8.5	9	9.5
5	36	40	44	48	52	56
6	44	48	52	56	60	64
7	48	56	60	64	68	72
8	56	60	64	68	72	76
9	64	72	76	78	84	88

The entire cuff and leg is knit in one flat piece with edge stitches to seam at the end down the back of the leg.

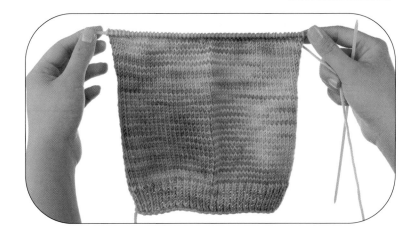

Knit the cuff as you would for top-down socks (see p. 65), in ribbing or another stitch pattern, turning your work at the end of each row.

If you are following a pattern that is designed to be knit in the round, you need to convert the stitch patterns to flat knitting—on wrong-side rows, stitches that are knits will be purled, and vice versa (purls are knitted).

TIP

Maintain 1 stitch at each end of the piece in stockinette stitch (knit on the right side, purl on the wrong side) for easy seaming at the end.

The instep is knit on half of the total number of stitches, from the side edge of the heel down to the toe in the center of the leg piece.

① Work across the leg piece until 25% (16 sts of a 64-st sock) of the stitches remain unworked. Place the remaining 25% of the stitches (16 sts) on a holder to work later for the heel.

② Turn the work and continue back on a total of 50% of the stitches (32 sts of a 64-st sock). Place the remaining 25% of the stitches on a holder to work later for the heel.

③ Work back and forth on these stitches until the instep measures 2 inches less than the total foot length, measured from the split point at the end of the leg. For standard measurements, refer to the table on p. 207.

You will work the top of the toe at the end of the instep, which you will seam with the bottom of the toe after you finish knitting.

Work a Basic Round Toe

1 Decrease for a Basic Round Toe as follows:

Row 1 (RS): K1, ssk, k to last 3 sts, k2tog, k1.

Row 2 (WS): Purl.

Repeat rows 1 and 2 until you decrease the number of stitches in the instep by 50%.

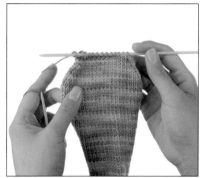

2 Work decreases every row as follows:

Row 3 (RS): K1, ssk, k to last 3 sts, k2tog, k11.

Row 4 (WS): P1, p2tog, p to last 3 sts, p2tog tbl, p1.

Repeat rows 3 and 4 until 1.5 inches' worth of stitches remain, between 8 and 14 stitches.

3 Place these stitches on a stitch holder or waste yarn.

Knit a Heel

For a flat sock, you can use the same heel patterns from a top-down sock knit in the round, including the gusset heel (see pages 66–71), or the short-row heel (see pages 116–123) from a toe-up sock. Both of these heels are knit back and forth no matter how you construct the rest of the sock.

Work a Gusset Heel

1 Return the held, unworked stitches at the bottom of the leg to the needles with the split in the center of the two halves. You will seam the back of the leg later.

2 With the right side facing, join yarn and knit a heel flap as for the top-down sock (see pages 66–67).

3 Work the heel turn at the bottom of the heel flap as specified in the top-down sock pattern. Cut the yarn, keeping the stitches on the needle.

4 Rejoin yarn at the right edge, at the top of the heel flap with the right side facing. Pick up the required number of stitches from the side of the heel flap, knit the held stitches from the heel, and then continue to pick up stitches along the other side of the heel flap.

5 Purl back across these stitches. Decrease for the gusset as specified in the pattern for a top-down sock (see pages 70–71).

CONTINUED ON NEXT PAGE

Work a Short-Row Heel

1. Return the held, unworked stitches at the bottom of the leg to the needles with the split in the center of the two halves. You will seam the back of the leg later.

2. With the right side facing, join yarn and begin working short rows as for the short-row heel on pages 120–123.

3. When picking up the wraps on the last pair of rows, simply turn the work and begin the next row after working the wraps together with the stitch—there is no following stitch to wrap.

Once the gusset heel decreases or the short-row heel is complete, continue knitting the sole even in stockinette stitch.

Knit the Foot and Lower Toe

1 Work the stitches for the foot even in stockinette stitch until the bottom of the foot matches the length of the instep to the beginning of the toe, or 2 inches less than the desired foot length.

2 Shape the bottom of the toe as for the top of the toe (see page 91). Place the remaining stitches on a stitch holder or waste yarn.

Sew Up the Socks

Once you finish the knitting, you need to sew up the sock into the proper shape, beginning with the seam at the back of the leg and continuing with the two foot seams. You will need a tapestry needle and a length of the sock yarn—or you can use doubled or thick sewing thread for a thinner seam (make sure your seaming yarn has the same washing instructions as your sock yarn). Mattress stitch creates an invisible, strong seam.

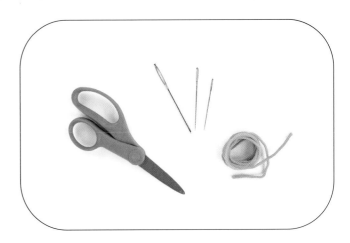

Sew Using Mattress Stitch

1. Thread the yarn (or thread) through the tapestry needle. Hold the sock so that the cast-on edge is at the bottom and the right side is facing you, with the edges of the leg close together.

2. Insert the tip of the tapestry needle above the cast-on stitch at the edge of the left piece, from underneath. Draw the yarn through, leaving several inches of tail.

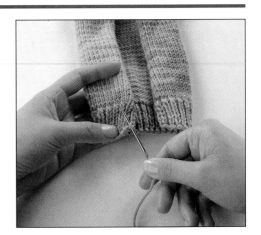

3. Insert the tip of the tapestry needle above the cast-on stitch at the edge of the right piece in the same manner, from underneath the work.

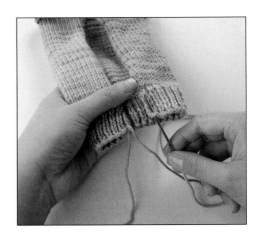

④ Return the needle to the left piece and insert the tip of the needle under one bar that runs between the stitches, from bottom to top.

⑤ Bring the needle to the right piece and insert the tip of the needle under two bars that run between the stitches, from bottom to top.

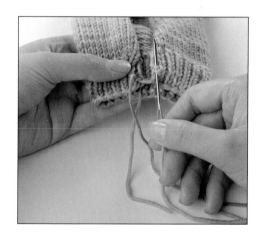

⑥ Bring the needle to the left piece and insert the tip of the needle under two bars, from bottom to top.

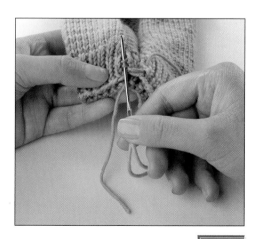

7 Continue to alternate between the two edges, inserting the needle tip under two bars each time. You do not need to pull the sewing yarn tight after each stitch.

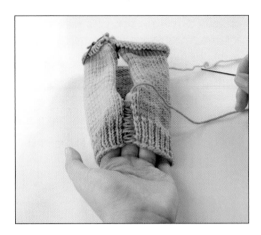

8 When you have completed about 1 inch of sewing, tug the sewing yarn to snug up the seam. The yarn should disappear between the stitches.

9 Once you have completed the seam at the back of the leg, break the yarn and weave in the ends (see "Weave in Ends," p. 42).

10 Sew the two side seams of the foot in the same manner as for the back of the leg, working down the foot to the held stitches at the tip of the toe. You might want to graft the toe (see p. 99) before completing the very end of the foot seams.

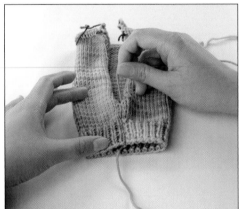

You can close the toe of a flat sock the same ways as a top-down sock in the round. Grafting the toe stitches produces a straight, flat tip, while gathering the toe stitches creates a more rounded tip.

GRAFT WITH KITCHENER STITCH

1. Return the held stitches of the top and bottom of the toe to working needles.

2. Graft the toe together with the Kitchener stitch (see pages 78–80).

GATHER THE TOE

1. Return the held stitches of the top and bottom of the toe to a working needle.

2. Thread a darning needle with a tail from the work. Work around the toe stitches, slipping each one purlwise onto the darning needle.

3. Once you have slipped all the toe stitches, bring the darning needle through all the stitches a second time in the same direction. Pull the tail tight and bring the end to the inside of the sock.

4. Weave in ends and block. You're done!

Basic Flat Sock Pattern

This basic pattern is for a flat sock in fingering weight yarn and employs the gusset heel and basic toe instructions. You can substitute a short-row heel (see pages 120–123) for the gusset heel.

Specifications

SIZE
Child M (Child L/W Sm, W Med, W Lrg/M Sm, M Med, M Lrg)

MATERIALS
200 (250, 300, 350, 400, 450) yd. of fingering weight yarn

US 1 (2.25mm) straight or circular needles, or size to obtain gauge

GAUGE
8 sts and 10 rounds = 4 inches square in St st

Pattern Stitches

FLAT 1 × 1 RIBBING
Row 1: * K1, p1 *, rep from * to * to end of row.

Row 2: * K1, p1 *, rep from * to * to end of row.

Rep rows 1 and 2 for patt.

FLAT STOCKINETTE STITCH
Row 1: Knit.

Row 2: Purl.

Rep rows 1 and 2 for patt.

Directions for Basic Flat Sock Pattern (Make 2)

1. Cast on 56 (60, 64, 68, 72, 76) sts using the desired cast-on method.

2. Work 1 × 1 ribbing until piece measures 1 inch from beg.

3. Continue even in St st until piece measures 5.5 (6, 6.5, 7, 7.5, 8) inches from beg or desired length to top of heel.

INSTEP

Work the instep over the center 28 (30, 32, 34, 36, 38) sts.

1. Next row (RS): K 42 (45, 48, 51, 54, 57) sts. Place last 14 (15, 16, 17, 18, 19) sts on a holder or piece of scrap yarn. Turn.

2. Next row (WS): P 28 (30, 32, 34, 36, 38) sts. Place last 14 (15, 16, 17, 18, 19) sts on a holder or piece of scrap yarn. Turn.

3. Work even on these 28 (30, 32, 34, 36, 38) sts in St st until the instep measures 5.5 (6.5, 7.5, 8, 8.5, 9) inches from the heel split, or 2 inches less than the desired foot length.

UPPER TOE

1. Row 1 (RS): K1, ssk, k to last 3 sts, k2tog, k1.

2. Row 2 (WS): Purl.

3. Rep rows 1 and 2 until 14 (15, 16, 17, 18, 19) sts rem.

4. Row 3 (RS): K1, ssk, k to last 3 sts, k2tog, k1.

5. Row 4 (WS): P1, p2tog, p to last 3 sts, p2tog tbl, p1.

6. Rep rows 3 and 4 until 6 (6, 8, 8, 10, 10) sts rem.

7. Place these sts on a holder or piece of scrap yarn.

GUSSET HEEL

Work the heel over 28 (30, 32, 34, 36, 38) sts.

1. Place 14 (15, 16, 17, 18, 19) sts from each side of instep onto one needle, with split at center. Join yarn with right side facing.

2. Row 1 (RS): * K1, sl 1 *, rep from * to * across.

3. Row 2 (WS): Sl 1, p across.

4. Rep rows 1 and 2 until you work 28 (30, 32, 34, 36, 38) rows in total.

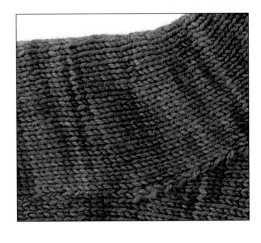

TURN THE HEEL

1. Row 1: K 16 (17, 18, 19, 20, 21) sts, ssk, k1, turn.

2. Row 2: Sl 1, p5, p2tog, p1, turn.

3. Row 3: Sl 1, k to 1 st before gap, ssk (1 st from each side of gap), k1, turn.

4. Row 4: Sl 1, p to 1 st before gap, p2tog (1 st from each side of gap), p1, turn.

5. Rep rows 3 and 4 until you work all heel sts, ending if necessary on the last rep with k2tog and p2tog.

6. 16 (18, 18, 20, 20, 22) sts rem. Break yarn, leaving sts on needle.

GUSSET

1. With right side facing, rejoin yarn at top of heel flap.

2. Next row (RS): Pick up and k 14 (15, 16, 17, 18, 19) sts along side of heel flap, k 16 (18, 18, 20, 20, 22) sts, pick up and knit 14 (15, 16, 17, 18, 19) sts along other side of heel flap.

3. Next row (WS): Purl.

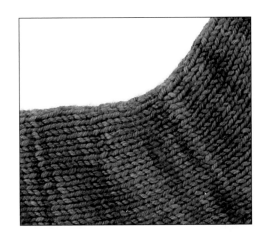

DECREASE FOR THE GUSSET

1. Row 1 (RS): K1, ssk, k to last 3 sts, k2tog, k1.

2. Row 2 (WS): Purl.

3. Rep rows 1 and 2 until 28 (30, 32, 34, 36, 38) sts rem.

4. Work even on these sts until piece measures 5.5 (6.5, 7.5, 8, 8.5, 9) inches from the back of the heel, or 2 inches less than desired total foot length.

LOWER TOE

1. Row 1 (RS): K1, ssk, k to last 3 sts, k2tog, k1.

2. Row 2 (WS): Purl.

3. Rep rows 1 and 2 until 14 (15, 16, 17, 18, 19) sts rem.

4. Row 3 (RS): K1, ssk, k to last 3 sts, k2tog, k1.

5. Row 4 (WS): P1, p2tog, p to last 3 sts, p2tog tbl, p1.

6. Rep rows 3 and 4 until 6 (6, 8, 8, 10, 10) sts rem.

7. Place these sts on a holder or piece of scrap yarn.

8. With yarn threaded on darning needle, sew center back leg seam. Sew foot side seams.

9. Graft or gather toe.

10. Weave in ends and block.

TIP

You can flatten the seams inside your flat sock to make them more comfortable. Turn the sock inside-out and cover with a damp cloth, then lightly press the seams with a warm iron.

6

Toe-Up Socks

Toe-up socks are worked just as they sound—the sock is cast on at the toe and then you work upward towards the leg. Toe-up socks are perfect when you want to maximize the length of your sock with no leftovers! If you are unsure how much yardage you have, toe-up socks enable you to get the most sock out of a limited amount of yarn.

Cast On and Knit the Toe

When it comes to toe-up socks, the cast-on and toe are the most involved steps. The Easy Toe and Eastern Cast-On use increases to shape the toe, while the short-row toe results in a slightly different look.

Cast-On Numbers

This table contains rough numbers for the cast-on of a toe-up sock when working an Easy Toe or Eastern Cast-On. Of course, you can adjust this number to suit your taste or foot shape.

Toe-Up Sock Cast-On Numbers	
Yarn Weight	*Cast On at Toe: Easy or Eastern (per needle)*
Worsted (5 sts/in.)	8
DK (6 sts/in.)	8
Sport (7 sts/in.)	10
Fingering (8–9 sts/in.)	12

TIP

For a wider toe, cast on more stitches in a multiple of 2—you will need fewer increase rows in the toe to reach the total number of stitches for the sock.

For a narrower toe, cast on fewer stitches in a multiple of 2—you will need more increase rows in the toe to reach the total number of stitches for the sock.

Easy Toe Cast-On

Using four double-point needles, The Easy Toe Cast-On incorporates a provisional cast-on (see pages 24–25) and several plain rows of knitting before increases begin to shape the toe. The Easy Toe can also be worked on one or two circular needles.

1 With waste yarn, provisionally cast on the number of stitches specified in the table on the opposite page for your yarn type. See "Provisional Cast-On" on pages 24-25 for two different methods.

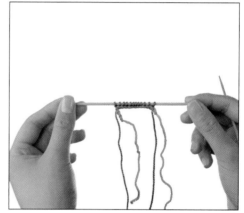

2 Work 4 rows even in stockinette stitch [knit 1 row, purl 1 row] twice.

③ Rotate the work so that the provisional cast-on is above the working needle. Pull out the provisional cast-on (waste yarn) and place the live stitches onto another needle.

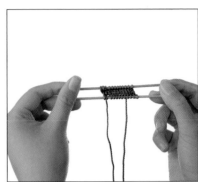

④ Rotate the work again so that the working yarn is attached to the right-hand side of the top needle. You will now begin knitting in the round.

⑤ Divide the stitches evenly over four needles by slipping half of the stitches off each needle purlwise onto new needles. Each needle should have the same number of stitches.

⑥ Increase as follows:

Needle 1: k1, m1, k to end of needle. Take up another empty needle.

Needle 2: k to last st, m1, k1. Take up another empty needle.

Needle 3: k1, m1, k to end of needle. Take up another empty needle.

Needle 4: k to last st, m1, k1.

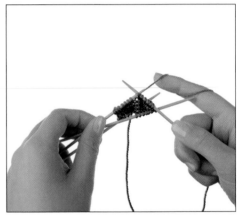

You have now evenly divided the stitches over four double-pointed needles and increased the total number of stitches by 4.

7 Place a split marker or piece of scrap yarn in the work to indicate the beginning of the round. Now begin alternating toe increase rounds with plain rounds.

Round 1:

Needle 1: K1, m1, k to end of needle.

Needle 2: K to last st, m1, k1.

Needle 3: K1, m1, k to end of needle.

Needle 4: K to last st, m1, k1.

Round 2:

All needles: Knit.

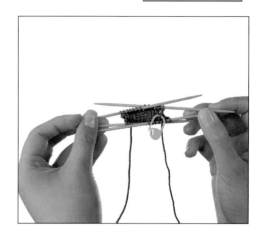

8 Repeat rounds 1 and 2 until you reach the total number of stitches in the sock, according to the table on p. 64 (top-down sock). The Easy Toe is complete!

CONTINUED ON NEXT PAGE

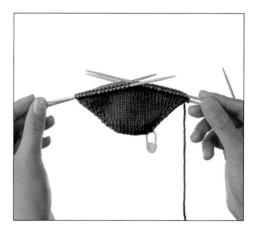

TIP

If you are working a pattern stitch across the top of the foot, make sure you have the correct number of stitches for the pattern repeat. If necessary, increase extra stitches across the top of the foot on the last plain round to provide the right number of stitches.

Eastern Cast-On

The Eastern Cast-On is an easy method that does not require a provisional cast on or waste yarn. It can be worked on double pointed needles (as shown here), one or two circular needles.

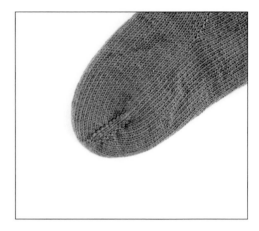

① Hold two double-pointed needles parallel in your left hand. The upper needle is labeled "A", the bottom needle is labeled "B". Catch the tail of your yarn between the needles, leaving several inches free behind the needles.

② Wrap the yarn under needle B and over needle A.

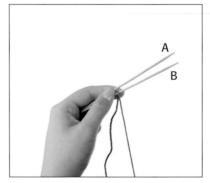
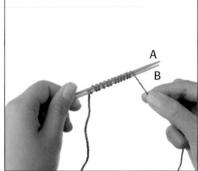

③ Wrap the yarn around both needles in this direction until you have the number of stitches prescribed for your yarn weight in the "Cast On Numbers" chart (p. 106), on both needles A and B.

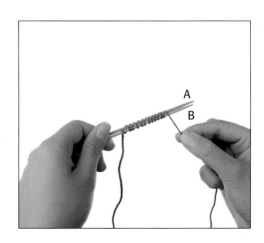

4 With an empty needle, knit the stitches of needle A by inserting the needle tip into the first stitch and between the two parallel needles, and then bring the working yarn below needle B to knit the stitch.

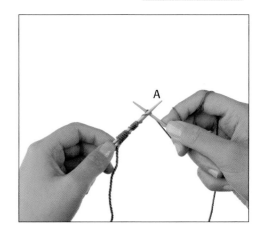

5 Once you work all the stitches on needle A, rotate the two needles 180 degrees so that the working yarn is on the right edge. Knit across the stitches on needle B.

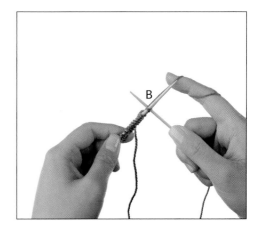

6 You are now ready to begin knitting in the round. Follow steps 4–6 of the Easy Toe Cast-On to divide the stitches over four needles and increase for the toe.

CONTINUED ON NEXT PAGE

Short-Row Toe

A short-row toe is knit in exactly the same manner as a short-row heel, beginning with a provisional cast-on.

① Provisionally cast on half the total number of stitches in the sock with waste yarn, following one of the provisional cast-on methods on pages 24–25. I recommend the crochet cast-on. For a 64-stitch sock, provisionally cast on 32 stitches.

② A short-row toe is constructed in the exact same way as a short-row heel. Follow the short-row heel instructions on pages 120–123 to form the toe.

③ Remove the waste yarn to release the live stitches from the provisional cast-on after you complete the toe. Locate the knot at the end of the crochet chain and undo the last stitch in the chain.

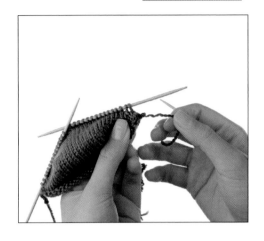

④ Pull the waste yarn (slowly) to release the live stitches, placing them onto an empty double-pointed needle as you go. Make sure you don't twist the stitches.

Once all the stitches have been recovered, divide the new stitches over 2 double-pointed needles.

⑤ Once all the stitches are on an empty needle, you're ready to continue in the round on the total number of sock stitches.

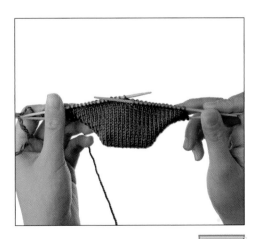

Once you have reached the total number of stitches for the sock, it's time to knit the foot.

CONTINUE EVEN FOR THE FOOT

For a simple stockinette sock, continue knitting even (without increases) in the round until the sock measures approximately 2 inches less than the desired foot length. See the "Sizing Chart" on p. 207 for a more precise chart of sizes.

ADD PATTERNING

Once you complete the toe, you can add any patterning you like. See Chapter 2 for more information on how to choose stitch patterns to incorporate into your socks.

Adapt a Top-Down Pattern

If you are adapting a pattern written for top-down socks into toe-up socks, you need to think about one major consideration: the pattern's direction.

IS THE PATTERNING DIRECTIONAL?

Many stitch patterns appear the same when knit in a different direction—ribbing, for example, looks exactly the same if knit from the top down – compare the ribbing on the Basic Top-Down Socks (p. 82) and the Basic Toe Up Socks (p. 134).

However, other types of stitch patterns do *not* appear the same when knit toe-up instead of top-down. If you follow a top-down pattern exactly, cable patterns appear to cross in the opposite direction than intended once you complete the sock.

Some lace patterns, such as those with diagonal lines, also appear to lean in the opposite direction than intended. Patterns such as leaves appear upside-down.

When working from a chart, you can adapt a top-down stitch pattern by reading the chart in the opposite direction—simply turn the chart upside-down to read. However, depending on the type of stitch, this might not work because stitches often depend on the preceding stitches—when working the chart upside-down, the rounds are in the opposite order as well.

FAQ

What patterns can be reversed easily?

Stitch patterns that contain only knit and purl stitches are easy to work in the opposite direction. If the pattern is square, like the Waffle Pattern of the Toe Up Thermal Sport Socks (p. 165), the texture will appear identical whether it is worked toe up or top down!

The heel in a toe-up sock is usually a short-row heel. However, if you like the look of the traditional top-down heel flap and gusset (see pages 66–71), you can create a similar looking heel from the toe up, too! Both methods employ short rows.

When working short rows, if you simply turn the piece around and knit, then holes form at the turning point. Wrapping the stitches fills in these holes for a smooth appearance.

How to Wrap and Turn (W&T)

WRAP ON THE KNIT SIDE

1 Knit to the point where you will wrap and turn. Bring the yarn to the front between the needles.

2 Slip the next stitch on the left needle to the right needle, purlwise.

3 Bring the yarn to the back between the needles.

4 Slip the stitch from the right needle back to the left.

5 Turn. The yarn is now correctly positioned to purl.

PICK UP ON THE KNIT SIDE

1 Knit to the wrapped stitch. The wrap is seen as a small bar across the bottom of the stitch. If you have two wraps, they are one atop the other.

2 Insert the right needle tip into all wraps from bottom to top, and then into the stitch on the needle as if to knit.

3 Slip all wraps plus the stitch to the right needle. Re-insert the left needle tip into all wraps plus the stitch, ready to knit.

4 Knit all wraps and the stitch together.

CONTINUED ON NEXT PAGE

WRAP ON THE PURL SIDE

1 Purl to the point where you will wrap and turn. Keep the yarn in front.

2 Slip the next stitch on the left needle to the right needle, purlwise.

3 Bring the yarn to the back between the needles.

4 Slip the stitch from the right needle back to the left.

5 Turn. To knit, you need to bring the yarn to the back between the needles.

PICK UP ON THE PURL SIDE

1. Purl to the wrapped stitch. The wrap is difficult to see from the purl side but you can easily visualize it from the knit side as a bar wrapped around the bottom of the stitch. If you have multiple wraps, they are atop one another.

2. Place the right needle tip through the wraps on the knit side from top to bottom. This will hide the wrap from the right side (outside) of the sock.

3. Lift the wraps up and place them on the left needle.

4. Purl all the wraps and the stitch together.

CONTINUED ON NEXT PAGE

Work a Short-Row Heel

You shape a short-row heel by using rows in which you don't knit all the stitches before turning—in other words, a "short" row. This type of heel looks similar to the heels on many commercially made socks, with a diagonal line running across the heel. You should work the method of short-row heel given here over 50% of the total stitches of the sock, using the "wrap and turn" method. Work this example heel over 32 stitches (half of a 64-stitch sock) on double-pointed needles.

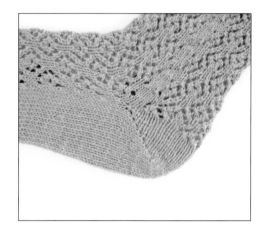

① Begin at the beginning of the round marker, which is at the side of the foot. Knit to the last stitch of Needle 1. Wrap and turn.

② Purl to the last stitch of Needle 4, working the stitches from both Needle 1 and Needle 4 onto one double-pointed needle. Wrap and turn.

③ Knit to 1 stitch before the last wrapped stitch of the heel. Wrap and turn.

4 Purl to 1 stitch before the last wrapped stitch of the heel. Wrap and turn.

5 Repeat steps 3 and 4 until the same number of stitches remains as cast on at the toe—8 (8, 10, 12) stitches unworked in the middle of the heel. Half of the heel is complete.

6 Begin the second half of the heel by knitting to the first wrapped stitch. Pick up the wrap and knit it together with the stitch. Wrap the next stitch, which now has two wraps, and turn.

7 Purl to the first wrapped stitch. Pick up the wrap and purl it together with the stitch. Wrap the next stitch, which now has two wraps, and turn.

CONTINUED ON NEXT PAGE

⑧ Knit to the double-wrapped stitch. Pick up both wraps and knit them together with the stitch. Wrap the next stitch and turn.

⑨ Purl to the double-wrapped stitch. Pick up both wraps and purl them together with the stitch. Wrap the next stitch and turn.

⑩ Repeat steps 8 and 9, working outward, until you pick up and work all wraps together with their respective stitches.

⑪ When picking up the wraps on the very last stitch of the heel, wrap the next stitch (the first stitch from Needle 2) before turning on the knit side, and wrap the last stitch on Needle 3 before turning on the purl side. The heel is now complete and you are ready to continue in the round on all stitches.

⑫ Knit across half of the heel with one double-pointed needle, then take up an empty needle and knit across the second half of the heel. Continue to knit around the whole sock.

⑬ Pick up the wrapped stitches on the last 2 rows of the heel and knit them together with the stitch as you come to them. This technique prevents a hole from forming at the very top of the heel.

CONTINUED ON NEXT PAGE

TIP

For a deeper heel, you can increase the number of stitches you use for the heel, up to 60% of the total number of stitches.

Toe-Up Heel Flap

A toe-up heel flap approximates the look of a traditional top-down heel flap and has a slightly different fit than a short-row heel. A toe-up heel flap is deeper than a short row heel, so you might need to experiment to figure out what heel fits your foot best. The example sock here is 64 stitches; you should treat different stitch counts similarly.

INCREASE FOR THE GUSSET

1 Work the foot until it measures approximately 3.5 inches less than the total desired foot length.

2 With the beginning of the round at the side of the toe, place markers for the gusset as follows:

3 Set-up Round: Work 32, m1, pm, work 32, pm, m1.

4 Work 1 round plain (without increases), maintaining any stitch pattern over the instep.

5 Work Inc Round as follows: Work to first marker, m1, sl m, work 32, sl m, m1, k to end of round.

6 Repeat last 2 rounds, alternating Inc Round and plain round, until you work the Inc Round a total of 16 times (32 stitches total increased, including set-up round).

SHORT-ROW BOTTOM OF HEEL

You work the short-row section that comprises the bottom of the heel back and forth, incorporating the wrap-and-turn method of a short-row heel.

1 Work bottom of heel as follows:

Row 1 (RS): K 31, w&t.

Row 2 (WS): P 30, w&t.

Row 3: K 29, w&t.

Row 4: P 28, w&t.

Row 5: K 27, w&t.

Row 6: P 26, w&t.

2 Continue in this manner, working 1 less stitch each row and wrapping and turning the following stitch, until:

3 Row 19 (RS): K 13, w&t.

CONTINUED ON NEXT PAGE

④ Next row (WS): P 13, work across wrapped sts by picking up each wrap and purling together with the st; on the last wrapped st, p3tog the wrap, st, and following st. Turn.

⑤ Next row (RS): K across, working across wrapped sts by picking up each wrap and knitting together with the st; on the last wrapped st, sssk the wrap, st, and following st. Turn.

DECREASE FOR HEEL FLAP

1 Decrease for Heel Flap as follows:

Next row (WS): Sl 1 pwise wyif, p 30, p2tog. Turn.

Next row (RS): Sl 1 pwise wyib, k30, ssk.

2 Repeat these 2 rows until you finish decreasing all the increased gusset stitches and 64 total stitches remain.

Toe-up gusset heel is now complete—continue to "Knit the Leg and Cuff"; see following section.

TIP

If you want to accommodate a larger leg, you can make the circumference of the leg slightly larger than the circumference of the foot by simply omitting the last 2 or 4 decrease rows in the heel flap. This change results in a larger stitch number for the leg.

Knit the Leg and Cuff

When knitting socks from the toe up, you can customize the length of the leg and cuff based on preference, fit, or yarn supply.

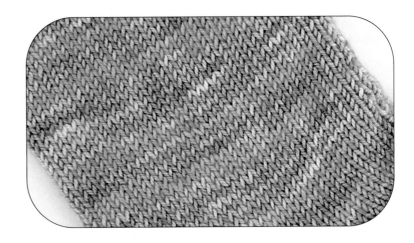

Basic Leg

Continue working in the round in stockinette stitch until the leg is approximately 1 inch less than the desired length.

Work 1 inch of ribbing or other cuff treatment of choice.

ADDING LEG PATTERNS

You can add many different types of stitch patterns to the leg of your sock – textured stitches, lace, and cable patterns are all fun to work and add interest.

The number of stitches in the stitch pattern repeat should divide evenly into your total number of sock stitches for a seamless pattern. You can also increase or decrease the number of stitches in the leg to fit your stitch pattern.

Cuff Treatments

You can greatly change the look of your socks by adding an interesting stitch pattern to the cuff. If you simply bind off a stockinette sock, you will get a rolled edge—great for casual socks, but it might not hold the sock up on the leg. Aside from the suggestions here, the cuff also lends itself nicely to lace edgings or other stitch patterns.

RIBBING

Ribbing is the traditional cuff treatment for socks.

For 1 × 1 ribbing, * k1, p1 * and repeat from * to * around. Repeat this round.

For 2 × 2 ribbing * k2, p2 * and repeat from * to * around. Repeat this round.

More complex ribbings include patterns with lace stitches, cables, or color work.

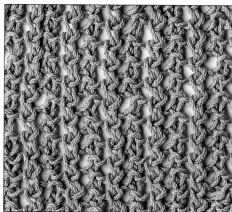

CONTINUED ON NEXT PAGE

PICOT EDGING

A picot edge is pretty and non-binding.

① Work even in stockinette stitch up to the top of the sock (work the total length).

② On the next round, work * yo, k2tog * and repeat from * to * around.

③ Work several more rounds plain in stockinette stitch (approximately 0.5 inches).

④ Bind off all stitches. Fold the edging at the eyelet round and stitch the hem in place inside the sock.

Binding off at an appropriate tension is important in toe-up socks. If the bind-off is too tight, it will be uncomfortable or perhaps impossible to get the sock on or over the heel.

Traditional Bind-Off

1 Work the first 2 stitches of the round in pattern.

2 With the left needle tip, lift up the first stitch on the right needle and pull it over the second, and then drop off the needle.

3 Work 1 more stitch of the round in pattern, making sure to leave the new stitch loose on the needle.

4 Repeat steps 2 and 3 until you have bound off all the stitches—1 stitch remains on the right needle.

5 Cut the yarn leaving several inches of tail and thread through this loop to form a knot.

CONTINUED ON NEXT PAGE

Stretchy Bind-Off

You can achieve a looser bind-off by using a stretchy form of bind-off—in this version, each stitch is knit more than once, resulting in a nonbinding edge.

1 On the bind-off row, k2tog, k1.

2 Place these 2 stitches back on the left needle without twisting, and k2tog, k1.

3 Repeat Step 2 to the end. When only 2 stitches remain on the left needle, k2tog and cut yarn. Pass the cut end of the yarn through the loop to finish.

TIP

Use a larger needle to bind off with, one or two sizes larger than your working needle, to make sure your bind off is loose enough.

Sewn Bind-Off

The sewn bind-off method is time-consuming, but the ultimate in a nonbinding edge.

1️⃣ Cut the tail of yarn, leaving about four times the the circumference of the sock. Thread onto a tapestry needle.

2️⃣ Bring the needle through 2 stitches from right to left, purlwise.

  Note: *As you bind off, keep the tension on the sewing yarn consistent.*

3️⃣ Bring the needle back through the first stitch as if to knit, and remove this stitch from the needle.

4️⃣ Repeat steps 2 and 3 until you have worked all the stitches.

Basic Toe-Up Sock Pattern

This basic sock pattern is written from the toe up in fingering weight yarn and a variety of sizes, with the easy toe cast-on and a short-row heel. You can substitute any of the toe and heel methods outlined in this chapter for the toe and heel in this sock.

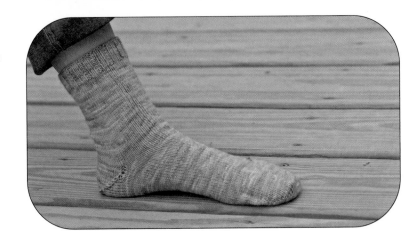

Specifications

SIZE
Child Med (Child Lrg/W Sm, W Med, W Lrg/M Sm, M Med, M Lrg)

MATERIALS
200 (250, 300, 350, 400, 450) yards of fingering weight yarn

US 1 (2.25mm) dpns, two circulars, or one long circular needle, or size to obtain gauge

GAUGE
8 sts and 10 rounds = 4 inches square in St st.

Pattern Stitches

2 × 2 RIBBING
Round 1: * K2, p2 *, rep from * to * around.

Rep round 1 for patt.

FLAT STOCKINETTE STITCH
Row 1: Knit.

Row 2: Purl.

Rep rows 1 and 2 for patt.

Directions for Basic Toe-Up Sock Pattern

EASY TOE

1 Provisionally cast on 10 (10, 12, 12, 12, 12) sts with waste yarn.

2 Work 4 rows in flat St st.

3 Rotate the work so that the provisional cast-on is at the top. Undo the provisional cast-on and place the live sts evenly onto 2 empty dpns. You are now ready to begin working in the round.

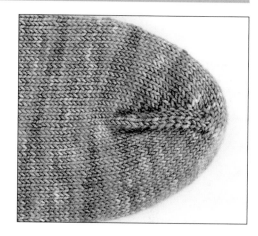

4 Round 1:

Needle 1: K1, m1, k 4 (4, 5, 5, 5, 5). Take up an empty needle.

Needle 2: K 4 (4, 5, 5, 5, 5), m1, k1. Take up an empty needle.

Needle 3: K1, m1, k 4 (4, 5, 5, 5, 5). Take up an empty needle.

Needle 4: K 4 (4, 5, 5, 5, 5), m1, k1. Take up an empty needle.

Place a marker in the work to indicate beg of round.

5 Round 2:

Needle 1: K1, m1, k to end of needle.

Needle 2: K to last st, m1, k1.

Needle 3: K1, m1, k to end of needle.

Needle 4: K to last st, m1, k1.

6 Round 3: Knit.

7 Rep rounds 2 and 3 as set until you have 52 (56, 60, 64, 68, 72) sts total.

CONTINUED ON NEXT PAGE

FOOT

Work even in stockinette stitch on these stitches until piece measures 5.5 (6.5, 7.5, 8, 8.5, 9) inches from the tip of the toe, or 2 inches less than desired total foot length.

Here you can incorporate different stitch patterns, such as ribbing, lace, or cables to add interest to the sock.

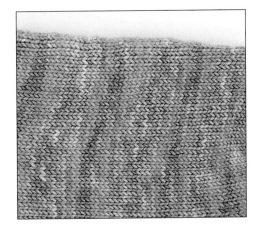

SHORT-ROW HEEL

Work the heel over 26 (28, 30, 32, 34, 36) sts. See "How to Wrap and Turn," pages 116–120.

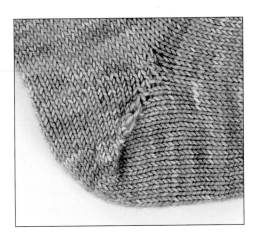

1. Row 1 (RS): K 25 (27, 29, 31, 33, 35) sts onto one needle. Wrap the next st and turn.
2. Row 2 (WS): P 24 (26, 28, 30, 32, 34) sts. Wrap the next st and turn.
3. Row 3: K to 1 before previously wrapped st. Wrap the next st and turn.
4. Row 4: P to 1 before previously wrapped st. Wrap the next st and turn.
5. Rep rows 3 and 4 until 12 (12, 14, 14, 14, 14) sts remain unwrapped in the middle of the heel.

PICK UP WRAPS

1 Row 1 (RS): K to wrapped st. Pick up wrap and work together with st. Wrap the next st and turn.

2 Row 2 (WS): P to wrapped st. Pick up wrap and work together with st. Wrap the next st and turn.

3 Row 3: K to double-wrapped st. Pick up both wraps and work together with st. Wrap the next st and turn.

4 Row 4: P to double-wrapped st. Pick up both wraps and work together with st. Wrap the next st and turn.

5 Rep rows 3 and 4 until you have worked all wrapped sts. On last pair of rows, pick up double wraps and work together with last heel st, then wrap the following st and turn.

6 Work 1 round even, picking up single wraps at sides of heel.

7 Work even on these 52 (56, 60, 64, 68, 72) sts until leg measures 4.5 (5, 5.5, 6, 6.5, 7) inches from end of heel or desired length of leg minus 1 inch.

8 Work 1 inch of 2 × 2 ribbing. Bind off all sts loosely using one of the methods from pages. 131–133.

9 Repeat all steps for second sock.

10 Weave in ends and block.

TIP

If there are any holes or gaps at the top of the heel, you can close them up by running a bit of yarn around the gap and tightening to close it up. Weave in the ends and block normally.

More Sock Patterns

Once you've conquered the basic socks, here are some more interesting patterned socks to try.

Slip-Stitch Ridges Socks

These top-down socks feature a twisted rib cuff, easy slip-stitch ridge pattern, an eye-of-partridge-stitch heel flap, and basic toe and are worked on double-pointed needles.

SIZE

Child Med (W Med, M Med)

Finished Foot Circumference: 6.5 (8, 9.5) inches

Custom Sizing: To vary the sizing, you can change the needle size to produce a different gauge. A tighter gauge will produce a smaller sock, and a looser gauge will produce a larger sock. Length is adjustable.

MATERIALS

1 (2, 2) skeins Lorna's Laces *Shepherd Sport* (100% merino wool, 200 yd./70g) in Lakeview

US 1 (2.5mm) dpns or size needed to obtain gauge
Tapestry needle

GAUGE

7 sts and 11 rounds = 1 inch square in St st

Pattern Stitches

1 × 1 TWISTED RIB

Round 1: * K1 tbl, p1 *, rep from * to * around.

Rep this round for patt.

SLIP-STITCH RIDGES

See figure at right.

Rounds 1 and 2: * K5, sl 1 pwise wyib *, rep from * to * around.

Round 3: Knit.

Rep rounds 1–3 for patt.

Directions for Slip-Stitch Ridges Socks (Make 2)

CUFF AND LEG

1 CO 48 (60, 72) sts.

2 Divide evenly over four dpns and join for working in the round, pm to indicate beg of the round.

3 Work 1 × 1 Twisted Rib for 1 inch or desired length.

4 Switch to Slip-St Ridges patt and work even until piece measures 5.5 (6.5, 7.5) inches from beg, ending with Round 1. End last round 12 (15, 18) sts before beg of the round.

EYE OF PARTRIDGE HEEL FLAP

1 Work the heel over 24 (30, 36) sts.

2 Row 1: * Sl 1 pwise wyib, k1 *, rep from * to * for 24 (30, 36) sts.

3 Row 2: Sl 1, purl across heel sts.

4 Row 3: Sl 1, *sl 1, k1 *, rep from * to * to last st, k1.

5 Row 4: Sl 1, purl across heel sts.

6 Rep rows 1–4 until heel flap is 24 (32, 36) rows long.

CONTINUED ON NEXT PAGE

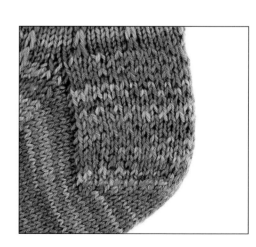

TURN THE HEEL

1 Row 1 (RS): K 14 (17, 20) sts, ssk, k1, turn.

2 Row 2 (WS): Sl 1, p5, p2tog, p1, turn.

3 Row 3: Sl 1, knit to 1 st before gap, ssk, k1, turn.

4 Row 4: Sl 1, p to 1 st before gap, p1, turn.

5 Repeat rows 3 and 4 until you have worked all heel sts, ending with a WS row. 14 (18, 20) sts rem.

GUSSET

1 Next round: Knit 14 (18, 20) sts. With the same needle, pick up 13 (17, 19) sts along side of heel flap.

2 Work in patt across 24 (30, 36) instep sts.

3 With an empty needle, pick up 13 (17, 19) sts along second side of heel flap.

4 With the same needle, knit 7 (9, 10) heel sts. Round now begins at center back heel.

DECREASE FOR THE GUSSET

1 Round 1 (Dec Round):

Needle 1: K to last 3 sts on needle, k2tog, k1.

Needles 2 and 3: Work instep sts in Slip-St Ridges patt.

Needle 4: K1, ssk, k to end of round.

2 Round 2: Knit.

3 Repeat rounds 1 and 2 until 48 (60, 72) sts rem.

4 Work in patt, maintaining Slip-St Ridges patt over instep and St st on sole, until work measures about 5.5 (7.5, 8.5) inches from back of heel.

SHAPE THE TOE

1 Round 1 (Dec Round):

Needle 1: K to last 3 sts, k2tog, k1.

Needle 2: K1, ssk, work in patt to end.

Needle 3: Work in patt to last 3 sts, k2tog, k1.

Needle 4: K1, ssk, k to end.

2 Round 2:

Needle 1: Knit.

Needles 2 and 3: Work in patt.

Needle 4: Knit.

3 Repeat rounds 1 and 2 until 24 (32, 36) sts rem.

4 Repeat Round 1 only until 12 (12, 16) sts rem.

5 Knit 3 (3, 4) sts. Cut yarn, leaving a 12-inch tail.

FINISHING

1 Graft toe with Kitchener st.

2 Weave in ends and block.

Worsted Boot Socks

These quick-knit socks are worked in worsted weight yarn and knit to a dense gauge. These top-down socks feature calf shaping by using a larger needle size, contrasting heel and toe, and a short-row heel.

Specifications

SIZE

W Med (M Med)

Finished Foot Circumference: 8 (9) inches

Custom Sizing: You can work this sock on any multiple of 4 sts. Length is adjustable.

MATERIALS

[MC] 1 skein Dream in Color *Classy* (100% merino wool, 250 yd./4 oz.) in Strange Harvest

[CC] 1 skein Dream in Color *Classy* in Blue Lagoon

US 5 (3.75mm) dpns

US 4 (3.5mm) dpns or size needed to obtain gauge

Tapestry needle

GAUGE

6 sts and 8 rounds = 1 inch square in St st on US 4 (3.5mm) needles

Pattern Stitch

2 × 2 RIBBING

Round 1: * K2, p2 *, rep from * to * to end of round.

Repeat this round for patt.

Directions for Worsted Boot Socks (Make 2)

CUFF AND LEG

① CO 48 (56) sts in CC with larger needles.

② Divide evenly over four dpns and join for working in the round. Place a marker for beg of the round.

③ Work 1.75 inches of 2 × 2 Rib.

④ Change to MC and work 1 more inch of 2 × 2 Rib (2.75 inches total).

⑤ Switch to smaller needles and continue even in 2 × 2 Rib until piece measures 8 inches.

SHORT-ROW HEEL

① Change to CC. Work the heel over 24 (28) sts.

② Row 1: Knit 23 (27), wrap the next st and turn.

③ Row 2: Purl 22 (26), wrap the next st and turn.

④ Row 3: Knit to 1 st before gap, wrap the next st and turn.

⑤ Row 4: Purl to 1 st before gap, wrap the next st and turn.

⑥ Repeat rows 3 and 4 until 8 (10) sts rem unworked in the middle of the heel.

CONTINUED ON NEXT PAGE

PICK UP WRAPS AND WORK THE FOOT

1. Row 1: Knit to the first wrapped st. Pick up wrap and knit it together with the st. Wrap the next st and turn.

2. Row 2: Purl to the first wrapped st. Pick up wrap and purl it together with the st. Wrap the next st and turn.

3. Row 3: Knit to the double-wrapped st. Pick up both wraps and knit them together with the st. Wrap the next st and turn.

4. Row 4: Purl to the double-wrapped st. Pick up both wraps and purl them together with the st. Wrap the next st and turn.

5. Repeat rows 3 and 4 until you have worked all heel sts and worked all the wraps together with their respective sts. Round now beg at the center back heel.

6. Change to MC.

7. Continue even in patt, maintaining 2 × 2 Ribbing over instep and St st over sole. Work foot to 7.5 (8.5) inches from back of heel (or 2 inches less than desired length).

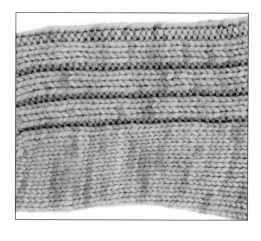

SHAPE THE TOE

1. Change to CC.

2. Round 1

   Needle 1: K to last 3 sts, k2tog, k1.

   Needle 2: K1, ssk, k to end.

   Needle 3: K to last 3 sts, k2tog, k1.

   Needle 4: K1, ssk, k to end.

3. Round 2: Knit..

4. Repeat rounds 1 and 2 until 24 (28) sts rem.

5. Repeat Round 1 only until 12 (16) sts rem.

6. Cut yarn, leaving a 12-inch tail.

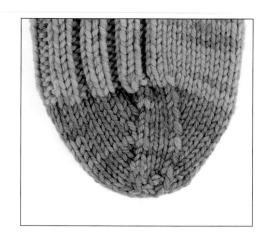

FINISHING

1. Graft toe with Kitchener st.

2. Weave in ends and block.

These top-down socks are worked in a variation of 3 × 1 ribbing. The slip-stitch heel pattern is carried through the heel turn and the toe is shaped in a swirl pattern. This stitch pattern works with any cast-on number that is a multiple of 4.

Specifications

SIZE

W Med (W Lrg, M Med, M Lrg)

Finished Foot Circumference: 8 (8.5, 9, 9.5) inches

Custom Sizing: You can work this sock over any multiple of 4 sts. Length is adjustable.

MATERIALS

1 (1, 2, 2) skein Dream in Color *Smooshy* (100% merino wool; 450 yd./ 4 oz.) in November Rain

US 0 (2mm) dpns or size needed to obtain gauge

Tapestry needle

GAUGE

9 sts and 12 rounds = 1 inch square in St st

CONTINUED ON NEXT PAGE

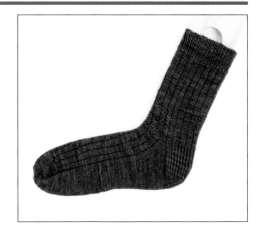

3 × 1 Garter Rib
Socks *(continued)*

Pattern Stitches

1× 1 RIBBING

Round 1: * K1, p1 *, rep from * to * around.

Rep this round for patt.

3 × 1 GARTER RIB

See figure at right.

Round 1: * K3, p1 *, rep from * to * around.

Round 2: Knit.

Rep these 2 rounds for patt.

Directions for 3 × 1 Garter Rib Socks (Make 2)

CUFF AND LEG

1 CO 72 (76, 80, 88) sts. Divide evenly over four dpns and join for working in the round. Place a marker to indicate beg of the round.

2 Work in 1 × 1 Rib for 1.5 inches.

3 Switch to 3 × 1 Garter Rib patt and continue even until leg measures 7 (7.5, 8, 8.5) inches from beg or desired length, ending with a round 1.

HEEL FLAP

1 Work the heel over 36 (38, 40, 44) sts.

2 Row 1 (RS): * Sl 1 pwise wyib, k1 *, rep from * to * for 36 (38, 40, 44) sts. Turn.

3 Row 2 (WS): Sl 1 pwise wyif, purl across heel sts.

4 Repeat rows 1 and 2 until you have worked 36 (38, 40, 44) rows.

TURN THE HEEL

1 Row 1 (RS): * Sl 1 pwise wyib, k1 *, rep from * to * across 20 (21, 22, 24) sts, ssk, k1, turn.

2 Row 2 (WS): Sl 1, p5, p2tog, p1, turn.

3 Row 3: Work in established slip-st patt to 1 before gap, ssk, k1, turn.

4 Row 4: Sl 1, purl to 1 before gap, p2tog, p1, turn.

5 Rep rows 3 and 4 until you have worked all heel sts, ending with ssk and p2tog if you don't have enough sts to end with k1. 20 (22, 22, 24) sts rem.

GUSSET

1 Next Round: K 20 (22, 22, 24) sts.

2 With the same needle, pick up and knit 18 (19, 20, 22) sts along side of heel flap plus 1 st in the corner at the top of the flap.

3 Knit across 36 (38, 40, 44) sts of instep (round 2 of Garter Rib patt as established).

4 With an empty needle, pick up 1 st in the corner at the top of the heel flap, then pick up 18 (19, 20, 22) sts along side of heel flap.

5 With same needle, knit 10 (11, 11, 12) sts from bottom of heel. Round now begins from center back heel.

CONTINUED ON NEXT PAGE

DECREASE FOR THE GUSSET

1. Round 1:

   Needle 1: K to last 3 sts of needle, k2tog, k1.

   Needles 2 and 3: Work in Garter Rib patt over 36 (38, 40, 44) instep sts as established.

   Needle 4: K1, ssk, k to end of needle.

2. Round 2:

   Knit.

3. Repeat rounds 1 and 2 until 72 (76, 80, 88) sts rem.

4. Continue even, maintaining Garter Rib patt for instep and St st for sole, until foot measures 8 (8, 8.5, 9) inches from back of heel, or 2 (2.25, 2.25, 2.5) inches less than desired total foot length.

SHAPE SWIRL TOE

1. Round 1: * K1, ssk, k to end of needle *, rep from * to * for each needle.

2. Round 2: Knit.

3. Repeat rounds 1 and 2 until 36 (40, 40, 44) sts rem.

4. Repeat Round 1 only until 16 (16, 16, 16) sts rem.

For mirror image on second sock, work Swirl Toe as follows:

1. Round 1: * K to last 3 sts on needle, k2tog, k1 *, rep from * to * for each needle.

2. Round 2: Knit.

3. Repeat rounds 1 and 2 until 36 (40, 40, 44) sts rem.

4. Repeat Round 1 only until 16 (16, 16, 16) sts rem.

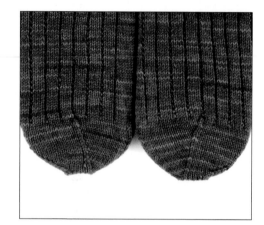

FINISHING

1. Graft toe using Kitchener st.

2. Weave in ends and block.

Cabled Cuff Socks

The cabled cuff of these top-down socks is knit flat as a rectangular piece, then grafted into a ring for the cuff. Stitches are then picked up from the edge of the cuff for the rest of the sock, which features a garter stitch short-row heel and garter stitch toe.

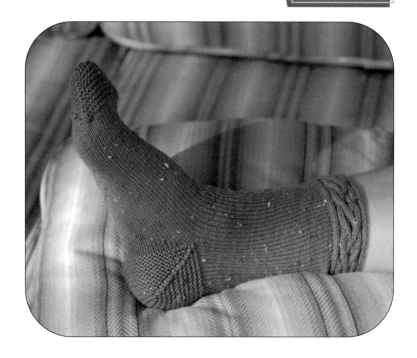

Specifications

SIZE

W Sm (Med, Lrg)

Finished Foot Circumference: 7.5 (8, 9) inches

Custom Sizing: You can work cabled cuff band to any length to fit around your calf. Pick up sts around cuff in a multiple of 4 to work leg and foot.

MATERIALS

2 (2, 3) skeins Knit Picks *Essential Tweed* (65% superwash merino wool, 25% nylon, 10% Donegal, 231 yd./50g) in Inca Gold

US 1 (2.25mm) dpns or size needed to obtain gauge

Smooth waste yarn

Tapestry needle

GAUGE

8 sts and 12 rounds = 1 inch square in St st

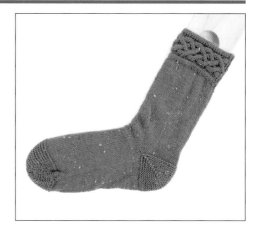

CONTINUED ON NEXT PAGE

Pattern Stitches

GARTER STITCH (KNIT FLAT)

Knit all rows.

GARTER STITCH (KNIT IN THE ROUND)

Round 1: Knit.

Round 2: Purl.

Re rounds 1 and 2 for patt.

Directions for Cabled Cuff Socks (Make 2)

CUFF AND LEG

Cabled band is knit flat on 2 dpns, then joined into a ring for the cuff.

1. Provisionally CO 20 sts with waste yarn.

2. Change to working yarn and knit 1 row on WS.

3. Next Row (RS): Knit, increasing 3 sts evenly across row. 23 sts.

4. Begin working Cabled Cuff chart (see chart at right). Repeat rows 1–16 of chart 5 (6, 7) times. Work should measure approximately 6.75 (8, 9.25) inches long.

5. Knit 1 row, decreasing 3 sts evenly across.

Chart columns numbered 23 22 21 20 19 18 17 16 15 14 13 12 11 10 9 8 7 6 5 4 3 2 1; rows numbered 1 through 16.

Legend:

(blank)	**Knit** — RS: knit stitch / WS: purl stitch
●	**purl** — RS: purl stitch / WS: knit stitch
V	**slip** — RS: Slip stitch as if to purl, holding yarn in back / WS: Slip stitch as if to purl, holding yarn in front
(cable symbol)	**cross 2 over 2 right/purl bg** — RS: sl3 to CN, hold in back. k2, sl center st from CN to left hand needle and purl it. k2 from CN / WS: none defined
(cable symbol)	**C2 over 1 left P** — RS: sl2 to CN, hold in front. p1, k2 from CN / WS: sl2 to CN, hold in front. p1, k2 from CN
(cable symbol)	**C2 over 1 right P** — RS: sl1 to CN, hold in back. k2, p1 from CN / WS: sl1 to CN, hold in back. k2, p1 from CN
(cable symbol)	**C2 over 2 right** — RS: sl2 to CN, hold in back. k2, k2 from CN / WS: none defined
(cable symbol)	**C2 over 2 left** — RS: sl2 to CN, hold in front. k2, k2 from CN / WS: none defined
(cable symbol)	**cross 2 over 2 left/purl bg** — RS: sl3 to CN, hold in front. k2, sl center st from CN back to left hand needle and purl it. k2 from CN / WS: none defined

6 Work in Garter St on these 20 sts until cuff measures 7.5 (8.5, 9.5) inches long, ending with a WS row. Cut working yarn, leaving a 10-inch tail.

7 Unzip provisional CO and place these 20 sts onto a working needle.

8 Thread tapestry needle with working yarn tail. Graft together live sts, forming cuff piece into a ring.

PICK UP STITCHES FOR FOOT

1 Place marker in work at midpoint of garter st section of cabled cuff.

Note: This might not be the grafted row of the cuff.

2 Pick up sts along knitted edge of cuff (slipped-st edge is top of sock) as follows: Pick up and knit in each of 2 rows along edge, skip 1 row.

3 Pick up 60 (68, 76) sts in this manner along edge of cuff.

4 Set up to work in the round and pm for beg of round, which is at the back of the leg.

Med and Lrg Sizes Only:

5 Next Round: Knit, decreasing 4 sts evenly around. (64, 72) sts.

Note: If your row gauge is slightly different and you pick up more or fewer sts along the cuff edge, decrease or increase on following round as required to obtain 60 (64, 72) sts.

6 Work even in St st until sock measures 8 inches from top of cabled cuff, ending 18 (19, 21) sts before end of round marker.

CONTINUED ON NEXT PAGE

SHORT-ROW HEEL

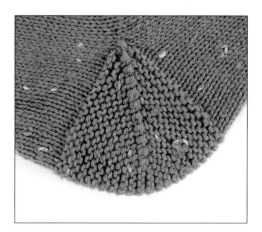

1 Work the heel over approximately 60% of the sock's sts—36 (38, 42) sts—and knit it in garter st.

2 Row 1 (RS): K 35 (37, 41) sts onto one needle. Wrap the next st and turn.

3 Row 2 (WS): K 34 (36, 40) sts. Wrap the next st and turn.

4 Rows 3 and 4: K to 1 before previously wrapped st. Wrap the next st and turn.

5 Rep rows 3 and 4 until 14 (14, 14) sts rem unwrapped in the middle of the heel.

Pick Up Wraps

1 Row 1 (RS): K to wrapped st. Pick up wrap and work together with st. Wrap the next st and turn.

2 Row 2 (WS): K to wrapped st. Pick up wrap and work together with st. Wrap the next st and turn.

3 Rows 3 and 4: K to double-wrapped st. Pick up both wraps and work together with st. Wrap the next st and turn.

4 Rep rows 3 and 4 until you have worked all wrapped sts. On last pair of rows, pick up double wraps and work together with last heel st, then wrap the following st and turn.

5 Work 1 round even, picking up single wraps at edges of heel.

WORK THE FOOT

1 Work even in St st until foot measures 6 (7, 8) inches from back of heel, or 2.5 inches less than desired total foot length.

2 Next Round: K 15 (16, 18), p 30 (32, 36), k 15 (16, 18).

3 Knit 1 round even.

4 Repeat last 2 rounds once more.

SHAPE THE TOE

① Round 1

    Needle 1: K to last 3 sts, k2tog, k1.

    Needle 2: K1, ssk, k to end of needle.

    Needle 3: K to last 3 sts, k2tog, k1.

    Needle 4: K1, ssk, k to end of needle.

② Round 2: Purl all sts.

③ Repeat rounds 1 and 2 until 28 (32, 36) sts rem.

④ Round 3: Work same as round 1.

⑤ Round 4

    Needle 1: P to last 3 sts, p2tog, p1.

    Needle 2: P1, p2tog tbl, p to end of needle.

    Needle 3: P to last 3 sts, p2tog, p1.

    Needle 4: P1, p2tog tbl, p to end of needle.

⑥ Repeat rounds 3 and 4 until 20 (20, 24) sts rem.

⑦ Sizes Med and Lrg only: Purl 1 round.

⑧ All sizes: P 5 (5, 6). Cut yarn, leaving a 12-inch tail.

FINISHING

① Graft toe using Kitchener st.

② Weave in ends and block.

Two-Needle Angora Baby Booties

These adorable booties knit up quickly in worsted weight yarn on two needles. You can adjust size by changing needle size or yarn thickness.

SIZE

3–6 months.

Finished Measurements: 3.5 inches from heel to toe

MATERIALS

2 skeins Lorna's Laces *Angel* (70% Angora, 30% lambswool, 50 yd./ 0.5 oz.) in Glenwood

US 6 (4mm) needles or size needed to obtain gauge

Tapestry needle

GAUGE

5 sts and 7 rows = 1 inch square in St st

Pattern Stitches

1 × 1 RIBBING

Row 1: * K1, p1 *, rep from * to * to end of row.

Rep row 1 for patt.

STOCKINETTE STITCH

Row 1: Knit.

Row 2: Purl.

Rep rows 1 and 2 for patt.

GARTER STITCH

Knit every row.

Directions for Two-Needle Angora Baby Booties (Make 2)

CUFF AND LEG

1. CO 32 sts, leaving a 6-inch tail.
2. Purl 1 row.
3. Knit 1 row.
4. Eyelet Row: * K1, yo, k2tog *, repeat from * to * to last 2 sts, k2.
5. Purl 2 rows.
6. Knit 1 row.
7. Work 4 rows 1 × 1 Rib.
8. Next Row: K 8, place these sts on a holder, k16, place last 8 sts on holder.

INSTEP AND UPPER TOE

1. Work back and forth on center 16 sts in St st until instep measures 2 inches from split.
2. Next Row: * K2tog *, rep from * to * to end of row. 8 sts rem.
3. Next Row: * P2tog *, rep from * to * to end of row. 4 sts rem.
4. Cut yarn, leaving an 8-inch tail, and place these 4 sts on a holder.

CONTINUED ON NEXT PAGE

SHORT-ROW HEEL AND LOWER FOOT

1 Place 8 sts from each holder onto one needle, with RS facing, so that back of heel is at center. Join yarn, leaving an 8-inch tail.

2 Row 1: K 15, wrap the next st and turn.

3 Row 2: K 14, wrap the next st and turn.

4 Row 3: K to 1 before previously wrapped st, wrap the next st and turn.

5 Row 4: K to 1 before previously wrapped st, wrap the next st and turn.

6 Repeat rows 3 and 4 until 6 sts rem unworked in center of heel.

7 Row 1: K to wrapped st. Pick up wrap, work together with st. Wrap the next st and turn.

8 Row 2: K to wrapped st. Pick up wrap, work together with st. Wrap the next st and turn.

9 Row 3: K to double-wrapped st. Pick up two wraps, work both together with st. Wrap the next st and turn.

10 Row 4: K to double-wrapped st. Pick up two wraps, work both together with st. Wrap the next st and turn.

11 Repeat rows 3 and 4 until you have worked all heel sts.

12 Work even in Garter st on these 16 sts until sole measures same length as instep (2 inches from end of heel).

13 Next Row: * K2tog *, rep from * to * to end of row.

14 Next Row: * P2tog *, rep from * to * to end of row.

15 Cut yarn, leaving a 4-inch tail.

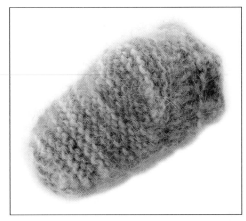

FINISHING

1 Sew back seam using 6-inch tail from cast-on.

2 Sew one side of foot using 8-inch tail from heel join.

3 Sew second side of foot using 8-inch tail from end of sole.

4 Place 4 sts from instep toe onto a needle. Thread 4-inch tail onto tapestry needle and thread needle through 8 toe sts. Pull tight and bring tail to inside.

5 Weave in all ends and block.

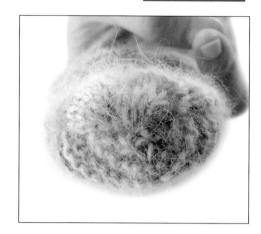

Make a Twisted Cord

1 Cut two lengths of yarn, 72 inches each.

2 For one cord, fold one length in half.

3 Holding one end of the folded length securely, twist yarn at other end in one direction until strand is tightly twisted (a).

4 Fold this twisted strand in half, allowing the two halves to twist around each other (b).

5 Knot halves together at each end.

6 Repeat steps 2–5 for other cord.

7 Thread twisted cord through eyelet loops of bootie, then tie securely in a bow.

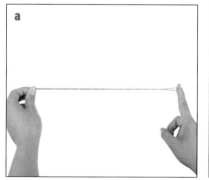

a

b

Toe-Up Floral Lace Socks

These toe-up socks use the Eastern Cast-On, a short-row heel, and a picot edging. Although only one size is given, the lace pattern is stretchy and accommodates a variety of sizes. You can also adjust sizes by changing needle size (a larger needle produces a larger sock) or yarn thickness (sport weight yarn produces a larger sock).

Specifications

SIZE

W Med

Finished Foot Circumference: 8 inches

MATERIALS

2 skeins Louet Gems *Fingering Weight* (100% merino wool, 185 yd./50g) in Mustard

US 0 (2mm) dpns or size needed to obtain gauge

Tapestry needle

GAUGE

7 sts and 9 rounds = 1 inch square in St st

Directions for Toe-Up Floral Lace Socks (Make 2)

TOE

1 CO 10 wraps (20 sts total) using the Eastern Cast-On.

2 Knit the sts on the top needle, rotate, and knit the sts on the bottom needle to complete the CO.

3 Round 1:

Needle 1: Kfb, k to end of needle. Take up an empty needle.

Needle 2: K to last st, kfb. Take up an empty needle.

Needle 3: Kfb, k to end of needle. Take up an empty needle.

Needle 4: K to last st, kfb.

4 Round 2:

Needle 1: K1, m1, k to end of needle.

Needle 2: K to last st, m1, k1.

Needle 3: Rep Needle 1.

Needle 4: Rep Needle 2.

5 Round 3: Knit.

6 Round 4:

Needle 1: K1, yo, k to end of needle.

Needle 2: K to last st, yo, k1.

Needle 3: Rep Needle 1.

Needle 4: Rep Needle 2.

7 Rep rounds 3 and 4 until you have 15 sts on each needle. 60 sts total.

8 Next round: K13, k2tog, k to end of round. 59 sts rem.

FOOT: BEGIN LACE PATTERN

1 Next Round: Work Floral Lace chart over next 29 sts, k 30 (see chart at right).

2 Work even in patt until foot measures 7.5 inches or 2 inches less than desired total foot length, ending at the end of Needle 2. Note the lace patt round on which you ended.

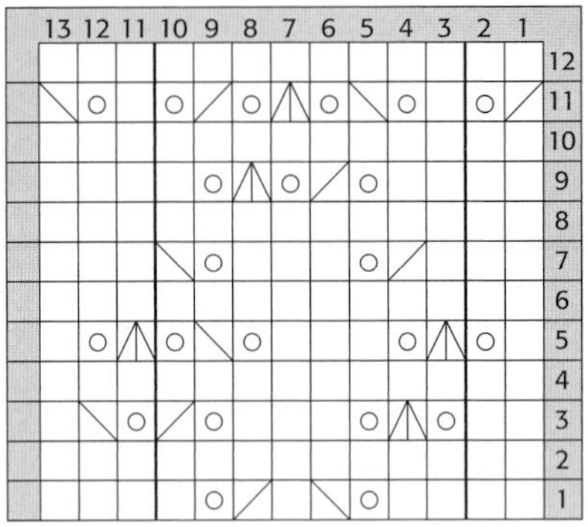

13	12	11	10	9	8	7	6	5	4	3	2	1	
													12
	○			○	╱	○	⋀	○		○		╲	11
													10
				○	⋀	○	╲	○					9
													8
			╲	○			○	╱					7
													6
○	⋀	○	╲	○			○	╱	○	⋀	○		5
													4
	╲	○	╱	○			○	╱	⋀	○			3
													2
				○	╱		╲	○					1

Legend:

☐	**Knit**	knit stitch
○	**yo**	Yarn Over
╲	**ssk**	Slip one stitch as if to knit, Slip another stitch as if to knit. Insert left-hand needle into front of these 2 stitches and knit them together
╱	**k2tog**	Knit two stitches together as one stitch
⋀	**Central Double Dec**	Slip first and second stitches together as if to knit. Knit 1 stitch. Pass two slipped stitches over the knit stitch.

SHORT-ROW HEEL

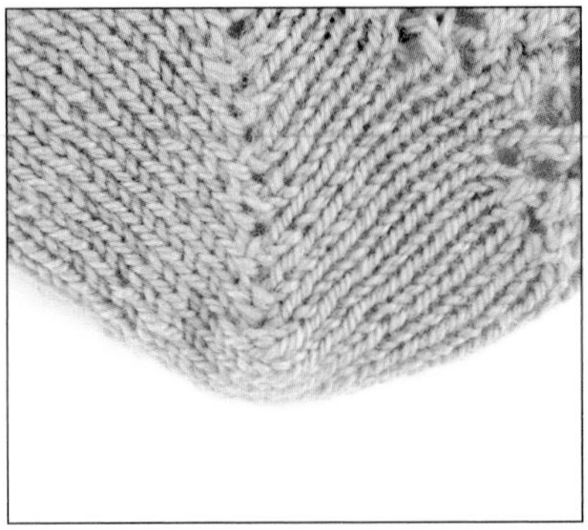

1 Work the heel over 30 sts.

2 Row 1 (RS): K 29 sts onto one needle. Wrap the next st and turn.

3 Row 2 (WS): P 28 sts. Wrap the next st and turn.

4 Row 3: K to 1 before previously wrapped st. Wrap the next st and turn.

5 Row 4: P to 1 before previously wrapped st. Wrap the next st and turn.

6 Rep rows 3 and 4 until 12 sts rem unwrapped in the middle of the heel.

PICK UP WRAPS

1 Row 1 (RS): K to wrapped st. Pick up wrap and work together with st. Wrap the next st and turn.

2 Row 2 (WS): P to wrapped st. Pick up wrap and work together with st. Wrap the next st and turn.

3 Row 3: K to double-wrapped st. Pick up both wraps and work together with st. Wrap the next st and turn.

4 Row 4: P to double-wrapped st. Pick up both wraps and work together with st. Wrap the next st and turn.

5 Rep rows 3 and 4 until you have worked all wrapped sts. Do not wrap after you pick up the last double-wraps.

6 Next Round: Work in Floral Lace patt over 29 sts, m1, k30. 60 sts.

LEG

1 Next Round: Work 29 instep sts (front of leg) in established Floral Lace patt, k1, work 29 sts (back of leg) in same row of Floral Lace patt, k1.

2 Work in patt on all sts, maintaining 1 knit st at each side and Floral Lace patt on front and back of leg until leg measures 6 inches from top of the heel.

PICOT CUFF

1 Work 6 rounds in St st (k all sts).

2 Picot Round: * Yo, k2tog *, rep from * to * around.

3 Work 5 more rounds in St st. Cut yarn, leaving a 24-inch tail.

FINISHING

1 Fold picot edge along picot round into sock and sew live sts down to inside, maintaining an even tension.

2 Weave in ends and block.

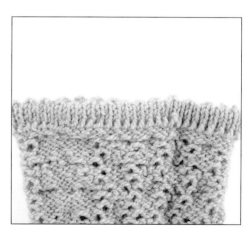

Toe-Up Thermal Sport Socks

These quick-knit, toe-up socks use sport weight yarn and consist of a stretchy waffle pattern with a short-row heel and twisted ribbing. Work these socks on double-pointed needles.

Specifications

SIZE

W Med (M Med)

Finished Foot Circumference: 8 (9) inches

Custom Sizing: You can use the waffle patt over any multiple of 4 sts. Length is adjustable.

MATERIALS

1 (2) skein(s) Louet Gems *Sport Weight* (100% merino wool, 225 yd./100g) in Teal

US 2 (2.75mm) dpns or size needed to obtain gauge

Tapestry needle

GAUGE

7.5 sts and 10 rounds = 1 inch square in St st

WAFFLE PATTERN (INSTEP)

Rounds 1 and 2: * K2, p2 *, rep from * to * around (for instep, end with k2).

Round 3: Knit.

Round 4: Purl.

Repeat rounds 1–4 for patt.

1 × 1 TWISTED RIBBING

Round 1: * K1 tbl, p1 *, rep from * to * around.

Repeat this round for patt.

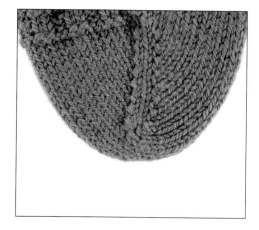

Directions for Toe-Up Thermal Sport Socks (Make 2)

TOE

1 CO 10 wraps (20 sts) using Eastern Cast-On.

2 Knit sts on the top needle, rotate, and knit sts on the bottom needle to complete the CO.

3 Round 1:

Needle 1: Kfb, k4.

Needle 2: K4, kfb.

Needle 3: Rep Needle 1.

Needle 4: Rep Needle 2.

4 Round 2:

Needle 1: K1, m1, k to end of needle.

Needle 2: K to last st, m1, k1.

Needle 3: Rep Needle 1.

Needle 4: Rep Needle 2.

5 Round 3: Knit1 round plain.

6 Rep rounds 2 and 3 until 60 (68) sts rem.

7 Next round: Work round 1 of Waffle Patt over 30 (34) sts of instep, k to end of round.

8 Work even in Waffle Patt over instep until piece measures 7 (8) inches from tip of toe, end with round 4 of Waffle Patt, beg heel with Needle 3.

SHORT-ROW HEEL

1. Work the heel over 30 (34) sts.
2. Row 1 (RS): K 29 (33) sts onto one needle. Wrap the next st and turn.
3. Row 2 (WS): P 28 (32) sts. Wrap the next st and turn.
4. Row 3: K to 1 before previously wrapped st. Wrap the next st and turn.
5. Row 4: P to 1 before previously wrapped st. Wrap the next st and turn.
6. Rep rows 3 and 4 until 12 sts rem unwrapped in the middle of the heel.

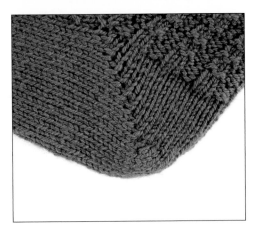

Pick Up Wraps

1. Row 1 (RS): K to wrapped st. Pick up wrap and work together with st. Wrap the next st and turn.
2. Row 2 (WS): P to wrapped st. Pick up wrap and work together with st. Wrap the next st and turn.
3. Row 3: K to double-wrapped st. Pick up both wraps and work together with st. Wrap the next st and turn.
4. Row 4: P to double-wrapped st. Pick up both wraps and work together with st. Wrap the next st and turn.
5. Rep rows 3 and 4 until you have worked all wrapped sts. Do not wrap after you pick up the last double-wraps.

LEG AND CUFF

1. Next Round: Work Waffle Patt over all 60 (68) sts.
2. Work even in patt until leg measures 4 (5) inches from heel.
3. Work 1 inch of Twisted Rib.
4. Bind off in patt.

FINISHING

Weave in ends and block.

Toe-Up Cables Galore Socks

If you love to knit cables, you'll love knitting these socks! These toe-up socks have cable on the instep as well as up the back of the toe-up gusset heel and leg.

Work these socks on one long circular needle with Magic Loop.

Specifications

SIZE

W Med (M Med)

Finished Foot Circumference: 8.25 (9.25) inches

Custom Sizing: Because these socks are patterned heavily, the easiest way to size up or down is to change yarn or needle size—thinner yarn and/or smaller needles produce a smaller sock, while thicker yarn and/or larger needles produce a larger sock.

MATERIALS

2 (3) skeins Lorna's Laces *Shepherd Sport* (200 yd./70g) in Pewter

US 1.5 (2.5mm) 40-inch circular needle or size needed to obtain gauge

Cable needle

Tapestry needle

GAUGE

7 sts and 10 rounds = 1 inch square in St st

CONTINUED ON NEXT PAGE

PATTERN STITCHES
2 × 2 RIBBING

Round 1: * K2, p2 *, rep from * to * around.

Rep Round 1 for patt.

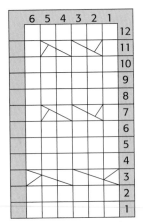

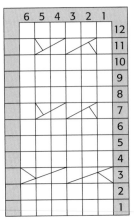

Legend:

	Knit
	knit stitch

	c3 over 3 left
	sl3 to CN, hold in front k3, k3 from CN

	c2 over 2 left
	sl2 to CN, hold in back k2, k2 from CN

Triple Cable A

Legend:

	Knit
	knit stitch

	c3 over 3 right
	sl3 to CN, hold in back k3, then k3 from CN

	c2 over 2 right
	sl2 to CN, hold in back k2, k2 from CN

Triple Cable B

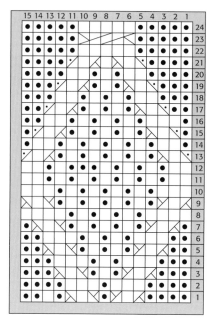

Legend:

	purl
	purl stitch

	C2 over 1 right
	sl1 to CN, hold in back. k2, k1 from CN

	C2 over 1 left
	sl2 to CN, hold in front. k1, k2 from CN

	knit
	knit stitch

	c2 over 1 left P
	sl2 to CN, hold in front. p1, k2 from CN

	c2 over 1 right P
	sl1 to CN, hold in back. k2, p1 from CN

	c2 over 3 right
	sl3 to CN, hold in back. k2, then k3 from CN

Diamond Cable (Left Sock)

Legend:

	purl
	purl stitch

	C2 over 1 right
	sl1 to CN, hold in back. k2, k1 from CN

	C2 over 1 left
	sl2 to CN, hold in front. k1, k2 from CN

	knit
	knit stitch

	c2 over 1 left P
	sl2 to CN, hold in front. p1, k2 from CN

	c2 over 1 right P
	sl1 to CN, hold in back. k2, p1 from CN

	c2 over 3 left
	sl3 to CN, hold in front. k3, k2 from CN

Diamond Cable (Right Sock)

CONTINUED ON NEXT PAGE

Directions for Toe-Up Cables Galore Socks (Make 2)

TOE

1 CO 10 wraps (20 sts total) using the Eastern Cast-On.

2 Knit sts on the top needle, rotate, and knit sts on the bottom needle to complete the CO.

3 Arrange needles to work with the Magic Loop–*Needle 1* refers to the first half of the round, *Needle 2* refers to the second half of the round.

4 Round 1:

Needle 1: Kfb, k to last st, kfb.

Needle 2: Rep Needle 1.

5 Round 2:

Needle 1: K1, m1, k to last st, m1, k1.

Needle 2: Rep Needle 1.

6 Round 3: Knit.

7 Repeat rounds 2 and 3 until 30 (36) sts rem on each needle–60 (72) sts total.

CABLE SET-UP ROUND

1 **Women's Size Only**:

Next Round: P2, k2, m1, k3, pf&b, k7, m1, k7, pf&b, k3, m1, k2, p2, k30. 65 sts total.

Men's Size Only:

Next Round: P3, k2, m1, k3, p3, k7, m1, k7, p3, k3, m1, k2, p3, k36. 75 sts total.

2 **All Sizes**:

See Cable Charts on pages 168–169.

Next Round: P 2 (3), work Round 1 of Triple Cable A, p 2 (3), work Round 1 of Diamond Cable (Left Sock), p 2 (3), work Round 1 of Triple Cable B, p 2 (3), k 30 (36).

3 Work even in cable patts on 35 (39) instep sts and work St st on 30 (36) sole sts until piece measures 6 (7) inches from toe, or 3.5 (4) inches less than desired total foot length.

INCREASE FOR GUSSET

1 Round 1 (Inc Round):

Needle 1: Work across 35 (39) instep st in patt.

Needle 2: K1, m1, k to last st, m1, k1.

2 Round 2:

Work even in patts on all sts.

3 Repeat rounds 1 and 2 14 (18) more times. 95 (113) sts total.

TURN HEEL

Work short rows over 30 (36) sts.

1 Row 1:

Needle 1: Work across 35 (39) instep sts in patt. Note chart patt row just completed (you will return to charts after completing the heel).

Needle 2: K 44 (54) sts. Wrap the next st and turn.

2 Row 2 (WS): P 28 (34) sts. Wrap the next st and turn.

3 Row 3: K to 1 before previously wrapped st. Wrap the next st and turn.

4 Row 4: P to 1 before previously wrapped st. Wrap the next st and turn.

5 Rep rows 3 and 4 until 11 (13) sts rem unwrapped in the middle of the heel, ending with a row 3.

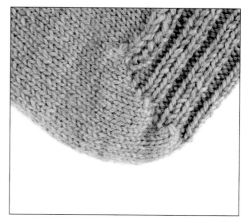

Pick Up Wraps

1 Next Row (WS): P 11 (13) sts. Continue purling across, picking up each wrap and purling it together with its st, to the last wrapped st. Pick up last wrap and p3tog the wrap, st, and following st. Turn without wrapping.

2 Next Row (RS): Sl 1, k across, picking up wraps and working each wrap together with its st, to the last wrapped st. Pick up last wrap and sssk wrap, st, and following st. Turn without wrapping.

CONTINUED ON NEXT PAGE

GUSSET DECREASES/HEEL FLAP

Women's Size Only

1. Row 1 (WS): Sl 1, p1, [k2, p2] across 24 sts, k2, p1, p2tog. Turn.

2. Row 2 (RS): Sl 1, k1, [p2, k2] across 24 sts, p2, k1, ssk. Turn.

3. Rep rows 1 and 2 14 more times. 30 sts rem on Needle 2.

Men's Size Only

1. Row 1 (WS): Sl 1, p1, [k2, p2] across 16 sts, [k2tog] twice, [p2, k2] across 14 sts, p1, p2tog. Turn.

2. Row 2 (RS): Sl 1, k1, [p2, k2] across 32 sts, p2, k1, ssk. Turn.

3. Rep rows 1 and 2 18 more times. 34 sts rem on Needle 2.

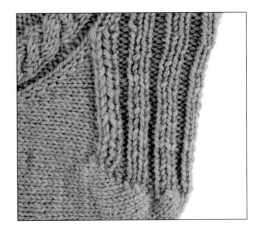

LEG AND CUFF

1. Work even on all 65 (73) sts in charted cable patts over instep and established 2 × 2 Rib over back of leg until work measures 8 inches or 2 inches less than desired length.

Women's Size Only

1. Next Round: P2, [k2, p2] three times, k2, p1, p2tog, [k2, p2] four times, work in established 2 × 2 Rib to end.

Men's Size Only

1. Next Round: P1, p2tog, [k2, p2, k2], p1, p2tog, [k2, p2, k2], p1, p2tog, [k2, p2, k2], p1, p2tog, [k2, p2, k2], p1, p2tog, work in established 2 × 2 Rib to end.

All Sizes

1. Work even in 2 × 2 Rib for 2 inches or until desired length.

FINISHING

1. Bind off all sts.

2. Weave in ends and block.

Toe-Up Cabled Knee Socks

Knee socks are ideal to work toe up, because you can try on the socks as you knit to ensure a perfect fit. The cables on these socks are on the instep and the front of the leg, but the calf is shaped along the back leg.

Specifications

SIZE

W Med (Lrg)

Finished Foot Circumference: 8 (8.5) inches

Finished Calf Circumference: Fits 14 (15) inches around widest part of calf

Custom Sizing: To shape the sock for a larger calf, work the calf increases more frequently (every second row) until you reach the correct size.

MATERIALS

2 (2) skeins Dream in Color *Smooshy* (100% merino wool, 454 yd./4 oz.) in In Vino Veritas

US 1 (2.25mm) dpns or size needed to obtain gauge

Tapestry needle

Covered elastic thread (optional)

GAUGE

8 sts and 12 rounds = 1 inch square in St st

CONTINUED ON NEXT PAGE

Pattern Stitches

1 × 1 RIBBING

Round 1: * K1, p1 *, rep from * to * around.

Rep Round 1 for patt.

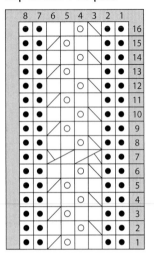

Legend:

Symbol	Name	Description
●	**purl**	purl stitch
□	**knit**	knit stitch
○	**yo**	Yarn Over
◹	**k2tog**	Knit two stitches together as one stitch
◺	**ssk**	Slip one stitch as if to knit, Slip another stitch as if to knit. Insert left-hand needle into front of these 2 stitches and knit them together
⬭	**c2 over 2 right**	sl2 to CN, hold in back. k2, k2 from CN

Scotch Cable A

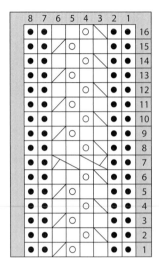

Legend:

Symbol	Name	Description
●	**purl**	purl stitch
□	**knit**	knit stitch
○	**yo**	Yarn Over
◹	**k2tog**	Knit two stitches together as one stitch
◺	**ssk**	Slip one stitch as if to knit, Slip another stitch as if to knit. Insert left-hand needle into front of these 2 stitches and knit them together
⬭	**c2 over 2 left**	sl2 to CN, hold in front. k2, k2 from CN

Scotch Cable B

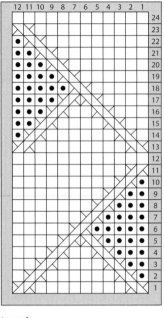

Legend:

Symbol	Name	Description
⬭	**LeftTwistEZ**	Skip 1st st, knit 2nd st tbl, knit 1st st, sl both sts off needle
□	**knit**	knit stitch
⬭	**RightTwistEZ**	k2tog, then k 1st st again, sl both sts off needle
●	**purl**	purl stitch

Sheepfold Cable C

Directions for Toe-Up Cabled Knee Socks (Make 2)

1. Provisionally CO 32 (36) sts with waste yarn.
2. Work Short-Row Toe as for Heel, working first half until 16 (16) sts rem unworked in the middle for toe, then working second half.
3. Unravel provisional CO and place live sts on needle. 64 (72) sts.
4. Knit 1 round even on all sts.

CABLE SET-UP ROUND

Size Med Only

1. Next Round: P4, k2, m1, k1, p4, k3, m1, k4, m1, k3, p4, k1, m1, k2, p4 (instep), k32. 68 sts total.

Size Lrg Only

1. Next Round: P5, k2, m1, k1, p5, k3, m1, k4, m1, k3, p5, k1, m1, k2, p5 (instep), k36. 76 sts total.

FOOT

1. See Cable Charts on pg. 174.

   Next Round: P 2(3), work Round 1 of Scotch Cable A, p 2(3), work Round 1 of Sheepfold Cable, p 2(3), work Round 1 of Scotch Cable B, p 2(3), k 32 (36).

   Note: For a mirrored cable on the second sock, begin Sheepfold Cable on Round 13.

2. Work even in cable patts on 36 (40) instep sts and St st on 32 (36) sole sts 7.5 (8.5) inches from the tip of the toe, or 2 inches less than desired total foot length.
3. End last round after instep sts and note the round you are on for each chart.

CONTINUED ON NEXT PAGE

Toe-Up Cabled Knee Socks *(continued)*

SHORT-ROW HEEL

Work the heel over 32 (36) sts.

1. Row 1 (RS): K 31 (35) sts onto one needle. Wrap the next st and turn.

2. Row 2 (WS): P 30 (34) sts. Wrap the next st and turn.

3. Row 3: K to 1 before previously wrapped st. Wrap the next st and turn.

4. Row 4: P to 1 before previously wrapped st. Wrap the next st and turn.

5. Rep rows 3 and 4 until 14 (14) sts rem unwrapped in the middle of the heel.

Pick Up Wraps

1. Row 1 (RS): K to wrapped st. Pick up wrap and work together with st. Wrap the next st and turn.

2. Row 2 (WS): P to wrapped st. Pick up wrap and work together with st. Wrap the next st and turn.

3. Row 3: K to double-wrapped st. Pick up both wraps and work together with st. Wrap the next st and turn.

4. Row 4: P to double-wrapped st. Pick up both wraps and work together with st. Wrap the next st and turn.

5. Rep rows 3 and 4 until you have worked all wrapped sts. On last pair of rows, pick up double wraps and work together with last heel st, then wrap the following st and turn.

6. Work 1 round even in patts, picking up single wraps at sides of heel.

LEG AND CUFF

1 Work even in patts until leg measures 6 inches from last row of heel. 68 (76) sts.

2 Next Round: Work 52 (58) sts in patt, pm for shaping, k to end of round.

3 Inc Round: Work in patt to 1 st before marker, m1R (right-leaning), k1, sl m, k1, m1L (left-leaning), k to end of round.

4 Work 1 round even.

5 Rep the last 2 rounds 3 more times. 76 (84) sts.

6 Rep Inc Round on next and every following fourth round 12 times. 100 (108) ts.

7 Work even until work measures 11.5 inches from top of heel.

8 Next Round: Purl all sts, decreasing 10 sts evenly around by p2tog. 90 (98) sts rem.

9 Knit 1 round even.

10 Purl 1 round even.

11 Work in 1 × 1 Rib until leg measures 14 inches from top of heel or to desired length.

12 Bind off all sts in patt.

FINISHING

1 Weave in ends and block.

2 If desired, thread some covered elastic thread through cuff ribbing to ensure snugness.

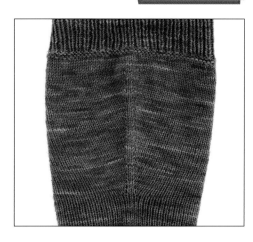

Troubleshooting: Fixing Mistakes

Sometimes, despite your best efforts, something goes awry in your knitting. From dropped stitches to incorrect sizing, you can always do something to fix a mistake. Even if you don't encounter a mistake until a round or two later, you can still save all your hard work!

A crucial part of knitting is figuring out when you make a mistake. You need to know how a split stitch looks compared to an incomplete or twisted stitch. Compare your work to the photos in this chapter and soon you'll fix your mistakes like a pro!

Unknitting

If you need to go back a few stitches or even a few rounds to fix an error, you can do so by *unknitting*, which is when you work backward and take out each new stitch and place it onto the left needle. This method minimizes the risk of dropping or losing stitches, especially in a complex stitch pattern.

① You make each stitch on the needles by drawing the working yarn through a stitch on the previous round. Identify a stitch from the previous round by looking just below the stitch on the right needle.

② Place the left needle tip straight into the front of the middle of this stitch on the right-hand needle. This places the stitch back onto the left needle.

3 Remove the stitch from the right needle (a). Pull the working yarn and it pops out of the stitch, leaving the stitch from the previous round on the left needle (b).

Repeat steps 2 and 3 for each stitch.

Note: *As you work backwards, you take yarn out of your knitting. If you go back a long way, wind your yarn back around the ball to prevent it from getting tangled.*

4 Move the yarn in front of the work when unknitting on a purl row (a). When you need to switch between knit and purl in the same row, move the yarn between the needles accordingly (b).

TIP

Even if you normally hold your working yarn in your right hand, pulling the yarn out of the stitches with your left hand is easier and faster when unknitting.

Dropped Stitch

A *dropped stitch* is one that has come off the needle. You might see it right away after you knit a round or you might miss it for a few rounds. Depending on the type of yarn you're using, the dropped stitch might just sit without going anywhere or it might "run," leaving a ladder behind. Luckily, you can easily pick up the stitch with a small crochet hook.

Pick Up a Dropped Knit Stitch

1 You can pick up a stitch that drops off the needle but doesn't run down by simply placing it back onto the left needle on the next round (a). Make sure that you place the stitch back on the needle in the correct orientation (b)—the front leg of the stitch should sit to the right of the back leg. (See "Twisted Stitch" on p. 190.)

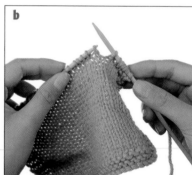

2 To pick up a stitch that drops several rows back, first identify the stitch. One strand of yarn runs between the adjoining stitches for each round that the stitch drops, which creates a ladder. Here, the stitch drops 5 rows (a). Knit to just before the dropped stitch.

3 Repair the dropped stitch by pulling each of those strands through the dropped stitch with a small crochet hook and working your way back up to the needle. Insert the crochet hook into the dropped stitch from front to back (b).

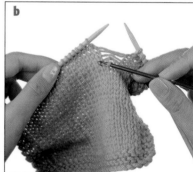

④ Catch the lowest strand of the ladder with the hook (a) and pull it through the stitch towards you (b). This technique moves the stitch up one round.

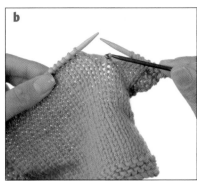

⑤ Remove the crochet hook from the stitch (a) and re-insert it from front to back (b). Catch the next strand of the ladder and pull it through the loop towards you.

⑥ Repeat Step 5 until you pick up all the strands and the stitch is level with the current round (a). Place the stitch back onto the left needle (b) and you're ready to knit again. Be careful not to twist this stitch.

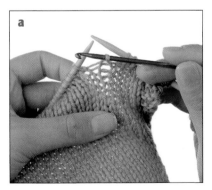

Pick Up a Dropped Purl Stitch

1 Because a purl stitch is the opposite of a knit stitch, you can pick up a purl-side ladder by working from the inside of the sock. Turn the work so that the inside of the sock faces you. Pick up the dropped stitch by inserting the crochet hook into the stitch from front to back (a) and pulling each strand through the stitch one round at a time (b).

2 To pick up a dropped stitch purlwise from the outside, you need to recreate the purl "bump." Arrange the dropped stitch so that the lowest strand of the ladder is in front of the dropped stitch.

3 Insert the crochet hook into the dropped stitch from back to front, and use the hook to pull the strand through the loop from front to back.

TIP

When you pick up the dropped stitch, the fabric might appear loose or elongated. Don't worry, any looseness will disappear when you wash or block your socks.

④ Remove the crochet hook from the dropped stitch and rearrange so that the next strand of the ladder is in front of the dropped stitch.

⑤ Repeat steps 3 and 4 until you work the purl stitch back up to the current round—and place it back on the left needle without twisting. Now you're ready to work this stitch again.

TIP

Laddering Down
Sometimes a dropped stitch can work to your advantage. If you notice an error several rounds down from your needles, you don't need to unknit or unravel back to that point. You can correct stitches by intentionally dropping a stitch, creating a ladder, and then picking up the stitch correctly.

Incomplete Stitch

As you knit along, you might encounter a strange-looking stitch. This stitch is incomplete—the stitch didn't quite make it onto the needle on the previous round. Fortunately, an incomplete stitch is simple to correct.

Complete an Incomplete Knit Stitch

1 Make sure that the stitch from the previous round is on the left and the loose strand is on the right.

2 Insert the right needle tip into the stitch from front to back, and pull the stitch over the loose strand and off the needle. The stitch is now complete.

Complete an Incomplete Purl Stitch

1 Make sure that the stitch from the previous round is on the right and the loose strand is on the left.

2 Insert the right needle tip through the stitch from back to front and slip the stitch to the right needle. Tip the right needle down slightly in front of the loose strand.

3 Push the loose strand through the stitch from front to back. Place the stitch back onto the left needle and now it is ready for you to work.

Did you accidentally knit a stitch instead of purl it, or vice versa? Did you also not realize your mistake until you're on the next round? Fixing this mistake is a variation on picking up a dropped stitch.

1 Take the incorrect stitch off the left needle. Gently pull the strand of yarn running between the two needles—this pulls the stitch out by 1 round.

2 Pick up the stitch correctly. For a knit stitch, insert a crochet hook or the tip of a knitting needle into the stitch from front to back and pull the strand back through the loop to re-form the stitch.

③ For a purl stitch, place the loose strand in front of the stitch. Insert a crochet hook or tip of a knitting needle into the stitch from back to front.

④ Pull the strand through the loop from front to back. Place the corrected stitch back onto the left needle.

TIP

Split Stitch

When working with some yarns, you can easily pick up only part of the yarn strand while knitting along. To correct a split stitch on the next round, take the stitch off the left needle and then replace it, taking care to place the needle through the entire stitch. To correct a split stitch several rounds down, ladder down and pick up the stitch in pattern, taking care to pull the entire strand through on each round when working back up to the needle.

Twisted Stitch

In a non-twisted stitch, the part of the stitch in front of the left needle appears to the right of the part of the stitch behind the needle. Sometimes, especially when picking up dropped stitches, the stitch ends up with the front leg to the left of the back leg, which creates a twisted stitch.

Correct a Twisted Stitch

You can correct a twisted stitch in two ways.

1 Take the stitch off the left needle (a), turn it, and place it back onto the needle—it is now untwisted (b).

2 You can also correct a twisted knit stitch by knitting into the back of the stitch rather than the front. Insert the right needle tip into the stitch on the left needle through the back loop from right to left—the right needle is behind the left needle (a).

Wrap the yarn as for a knit stitch and pull the new stitch through from back to front. The stitch is now untwisted and correctly mounted for the next round (b).

The *right side* of the work is the side that faces out—in a stockinette-stitch sock, it is the smooth side and is composed of V-shaped stitches. The bumpy side faces inward. However, you might find that rather than appearing on the outside of the tube, your right side is showing up on the inside. You are knitting inside out!

Switch to Right Side Out

① Push the work through the middle of the tube to switch from knitting inside out to right side out. Although the end result of the fabric is the same as knitting right side out, when working heels, toes, or any complex patterning, make sure you have the right side of the work on the outside of the tube.

② To prevent yourself from knitting inside out, always work on the needles closest to you, with the work behind. If the work is between you and the needles, you are likely working inside out.

Laddering

When working in the round on double-points, two circular, or one long circular, sometimes "gaps" or "ladders" form at the junction of two needles. Pulling the needles in opposite directions creates tension on the stitches, which causes a gap.

Cause and Prevention

The laddering effect is often more pronounced when using double-pointed needles because there are more junctions—four rather than the two you get when working with circulars.

To prevent ladders, pull the working yarn firmly on the first 2 stitches when switching needles. This helps to tighten the corners.

Shift the Stitches

If you are still having trouble, try shifting the stitches from needle to needle as you knit around. This prevents a ladder effect because you disperse the loose stitches over the entire sock. However, some patterns assume that the stitches on each needle remain on the same needle for the course of the sock. Just make sure your stitches are on the right needles when knitting a heel or toe.

1 Knit to the last 2 stitches of the needle (double-pointed or circular).

2 Slip the last 2 stitches onto the next needle, taking care not to twist them, then knit across the next needle as usual to the last 2 stitches.

3 Repeat Step 2 as you go around to shift the stitches from needle to needle.

chapter

9

Care for Your Socks

Once the knitting's done, you can finally use those hand-knit socks!
Keeping your socks in top condition is the key to a long and useful life.
Wash and store your hand-knit socks carefully, and you'll have them for
years to come. Inevitably, though, with time comes age, and your socks
might need a few repairs to keep them going.

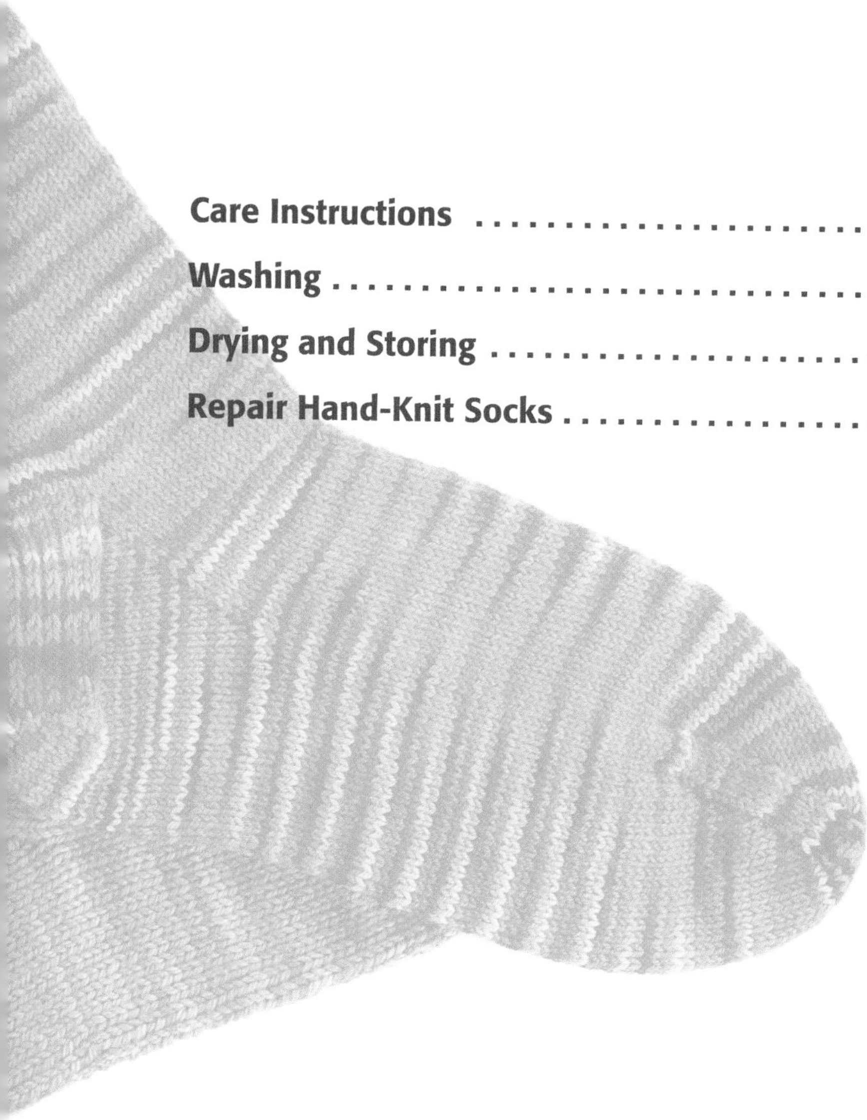

Washing instructions depend on the type of yarn you use—different fibers require different care. Many yarn labels carry both written instructions and care symbols.

Hand Wash

Hand Wash

You should gently wash items made from this yarn. Some washing machines have an acceptable "hand-wash" setting that mimics actual hand-washing, but you should test this cycle on a swatch before throwing in your whole project. For a yarn made of animal fiber, this symbol indicates that the yarn will felt and shrink if washed in a washing machine.

Machine Wash

Normal   Delicate/Gentle   Cool/Cold   Warm   Hot

The symbol for machine washing usually shows a temperature or temperature range that is acceptable for the yarn, from cool to warm. On a wool or animal fiber yarn, this symbol indicates that the fiber has been treated to prevent felting when machine washed.

Do Not Wash/ Dry Clean Only

Do Not Wash   Dry Clean

An X through any symbol means that the operation is not recommended. A "Do Not Wash" symbol is often accompanied by a symbol indicating that dry cleaning is required.

Tumble Dry

Tumble Dry, Normal

You can place fabric made from this yarn in the dryer. Many machine-dryable yarns recommend removing the item from the dryer when damp and laying flat until it is completely dry.

Dry Flat

Dry Flat

After you wash the item, lay it out flat to dry. Placing the item in the dryer might result in shrinkage. Hanging the item to dry, especially with larger items, can result in stretching. You can dry flat on a sweater rack or on a towel on a flat surface.

Warm Iron/ Do Not Iron

Do Not Iron   Low   Medium   High

Pressing your knitted item is one way of blocking the piece and giving it a professional finish. However, use caution when pressing or steaming. Yarns that contain a high proportion of synthetic materials such as polyester or acrylic can melt under the heat of an iron, "killing" the fabric and making it limp. Be sure to use a pressing cloth when ironing any item and only press lightly.

How often you wash your hand-knit socks depends mainly on how often you wear them. Some people wear their socks several times before washing, while others wash their socks after every wearing. Either way, you need to wash them in a manner appropriate to the yarn you used.

Dishwashing liquid and normal shampoo are great detergents to use when hand-washing your socks. Avoid harsh detergents, because they can alter the feel of the fabric after washing.

Hand-Wash with Soap

1 Fill a tub or sink with tepid water and mix in some detergent. Submerge the socks, holding them under the water until they are wet (a).

2 Soak for ten minutes, then drain the tub or sink. Refill with plain, tepid water and soak again, swishing the socks gently to remove the detergent (b).

3 Soak for at least five minutes; drain again. If the socks still feel soapy, rinse again in clean water. Remove your socks and squeeze gently to remove most of the water—don't wring.

4 Roll the socks up in a small towel and press to remove excess dampness. See "Drying and Storing" on p. 200 for instructions on how to dry your newly washed socks.

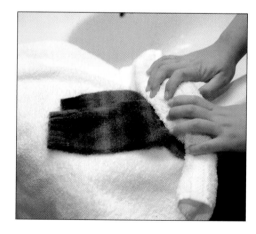

Hand-Wash with Wool Wash

Several products on the market cater specifically to knitters who hand-wash. These no-rinse *wool washes* are designed to clean and soften wool and other natural fibers quickly and easily.

1 Fill a tub or sink large enough to hold your socks with tepid water and mix in a small amount of wool wash—usually 1 teaspoon (5ml) works well for one pair of socks. Place your socks in the wash, holding them under until the fabric is wet.

2 Soak for ten to fifteen minutes, then remove from the wash and squeeze out excess water without wringing. See "Drying and Storing" on p. 200 for instructions on how to dry your newly washed socks.

TIP

No-rinse wool washes soften animal fibers because they contain lanolin; however, the lanolin can leave a residue on cotton or silk fibers. To avoid this, rinse non-animal fibers in plain water before drying.

Machine Wash Your Socks

If the yarn's label indicates that the yarn is machine washable, then you can include your socks in your normal laundry provided you are washing in the temperature indicated. If a washing temperature is not given on the label, a cold-water wash is gentler than a hot one.

Sort your socks according to color. You should wash bright or dark colors separately the first time (either in the machine or by hand) in case the color bleeds.

TIP

To prolong the life of your socks, launder them on a gentle or hand-wash cycle in your washing machine. You can also place your socks in a mesh laundry bag to protect them and prevent excess agitation.

Dry your socks according to the care instructions on your sock yarn. If you are in doubt, dry the socks flat. Store your hand-knit socks carefully to keep them from becoming misshapen or worse, attractive to moths. Always store your socks clean. Moths prefer fabrics that are worn. Unfortunately, once moths get in, getting them out is difficult. Carefully sort through any other nearby woolens or fabrics and take out any affected material. The best protection is vigilance!

If the yarn is not machine-dryable, lay the socks out flat on a towel or other clean surface to dry. Because socks are small, they tend to dry quickly.

If the yarn is machine-dryable, tumble the socks on a warm setting and remove before completely dry, laying them flat to dry completely. Because of the agitation in the dryer, machine drying can shorten the life of your hand-knit socks—laying them out to dry is gentler on the fabric.

 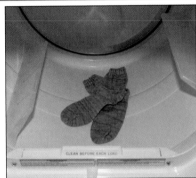

You can also hang your socks to dry. Because socks are small and fairly light, gravity won't pull down and misshape your socks. Hanging socks to dry allows air to circulate around them, drying them quickly. You can hang your drying socks over a clothes hanger or laundry drying rack, or even over the shower curtain rod.

To deter moths and other undesirables, place a sachet of eucalyptus, dried lavender, or cedar shavings among your knits—moths dislike strong smells. You can also purchase small cedar balls or flat pieces to tuck into your hand-knits drawer.

Note: Don't pull one cuff over the other to keep the pairs together. This stretches out the fibers over time, leaving one cuff bigger or less elastic. Instead, stack the socks one atop the other and roll them up together.

Eventually, you might need to repair your hand-knit socks. Wear from friction with shoes or hard floors can cause thinning, weakening, and eventually breakage in the fabric. You can prolong the life of your socks by reinforcing thinning fabric or repair holes with darning.

Duplicate Stitch

1 Inspect your hand-knit socks often once you've worn them a few times—it is much easier to stop or repair smaller damage. You can reinforce a thinning section with duplicate stitch.

With doubled sewing thread or matching yarn, thread a darning needle and leave the end unknotted. Begin at the bottom right corner of the section you wish to duplicate stitch with the right side facing you—you will work in rows from right to left. You will duplicate stitch a patch that is slightly larger than the actual thinning section, at least one or two stitches in all directions.

2 Insert the tip of the needle through the fabric from back to front in the base of the stitch you're covering.

3 Insert the tip of the needle from right to left behind both legs of the stitch in the row above.

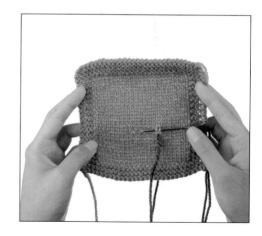

4 Insert the needle back into the base of the stitch, in the same place where the needle initially came out. One stitch is now covered.

5 Bring the needle tip up through the base of the next stitch to the left. Repeat steps 2–4 to cover this stitch.

6 Work across until you cover the entire width of the patch. Turn the work upside down and work the next row from right to left (a).

7 Continue duplicate stitching over the thinning section until you cover it completely (b). Weave in the ends.

a

b

Darn a Patch

Once your sock has an actual hole, you need to repair the fabric by creating a patch of fabric using sewing thread or strong yarn.

① Begin about ½ inch from the right edge of the hole and ½ inch below it. Insert the threaded needle through the work, then make short vertical running stitches up to ½ inch past the top of the hole.

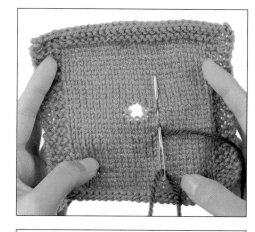

② Turn the work upside down and make another row of running stitches next to the first, closer to the hole. Continue repeating these rows until you reach the actual open section.

③ Insert the needle tip into fabric above or below the hole, then take the thread across the gap and insert the needle into the fabric on the other side.

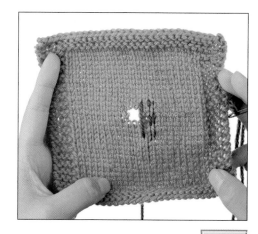

4 Turn the work upside down and make another strand across the hole next to the first (a). Place the strands fairly close together to produce a tight fabric when completed.

5 Continue to work across the gap until you reach the other side, then do several rows of running stitches through the whole fabric on the other side of the gap (b).

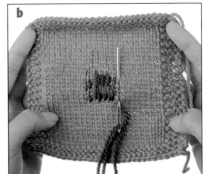

6 Turn the work 90 degrees so that the strands across the gap now run from left to right. Make several rows of running stitches in the intact fabric to the side of the gap to anchor the patch.

7 When you are ready to begin weaving the patch, take several running stitches vertically to get to the gap. Then use the needle tip to weave the thread under and over the gap threads, creating a woven section.

⑧ Take several running stitches in the fabric on the other side of the gap. Turn the work upside down and work across the gap threads again. This time, alternate the threads that you work under and over—you should now work over the threads that the needle passed under in the previous row and vice versa. Take several running stitches in the fabric beyond the gap and turn the work again.

⑨ Continue weaving back and forth until you fill the entire open section with the woven patch. The threads are close together for a long-lasting patch. Work several rows of running stitches in the last edge of the patch and secure the ends.

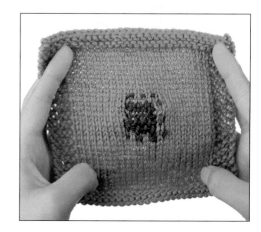

FAQ

What else can I do to cover a hole in my socks?
If you don't want to darn a patch directly into your socks, or if you don't have matching yarn, you can simply knit a patch. Work a piece of fabric in stockinette stitch (or your pattern stitch) large enough to cover the hole by ¼ inch all around, and sew the patch firmly into place over the hole with sewing thread.

Abbreviations

Abbreviation	Meaning
approx	approximately
beg	begin[ning]
BO	bind off [cast off]
CC	contrasting color
cn	cable needle
CO	cast on
dec	decrease[ing]
dpn	double pointed needles[s]
g	grams
inc	increase[ing]
k	knit
k tbl	knit through back of loop
k2tog	knit two together
k3tog	knit three together
kfb	knit into front and back of stitch
kwise	knitwise (as if to knit)
MC	main color
m1	make 1 increase (knitwise unless otherwise specified)
mm	millimeters
oz	ounces
p	purl
p2tog	purl two together
p3tog	purl three together
patt[s]	pattern[s]

Abbreviation	Meaning
pfb	purl into front and back of stitch
pm	place marker
psso	pass slipped stitch[es] over
pwise	purlwise (as if to purl)
rem	remaining
rep	repeat
RS	right side[s]
rnd[s]	round[s]
SK2P	slip 1 stitch, knit two together, pass slipped stitch over
ssk	slip 2 stitches as if to knit, then knit those 2 stitches together
ssp	slip 2 stitches as if to purl, then purl those 2 stitches together
sl	slip
sl st	slip stitch
st[s]	stitch[es]
St st	stockinette stitch
tog	together
WS	wrong side[s]
wyib	with yarn in back
wyif	with yarn in front
w&t	wrap and turn
YO	yarn over
* *	repeat directions between ** as many times as indicated

Sizing Chart and Yarn Requirements

Foot sizing is extremely variable, particularly foot length. Luckily, handknit socks are extremely stretchy and can accommodate a variety of sizes. Your yardage requirements will vary depending on the style and pattern of the socks you knit, the size of the socks, and the thickness of the yarn. This table gives you a good idea of how much yarn to buy to make a pair of socks.

Standard US Shoe Sizes with Measurements and Lengths				
US Size	Eur Size	Sock Size	Foot Circumference (in)	Foot Length (in)
C 7–8	23–24	Child's S	5.5	6
C 9–11	25–28	Child's M	6.5	7
W/M 1–3	30–34	Child's L	7	8
W 5–7	36–38	Women's S	7.5	8.5
W 7.5–8.5	39–40	Women's M	8	9.5
W 9–11	41–42	Women's L	8.5	10.25
M 7–8.5	40–42	Men's S	9	10.5
M 9–10	43–44	Men's M	9.5	11
M 11–12	45–46	Men's L	10	11.5

Approximate Yardage Requirements by Size and Gauge						
Gauge(Sts/in)	Child M	Child L/Women S	Women M	Women L/Men S	Men M	Men L
5	150	200	225	300	325	350
6	160	220	250	310	330	375
7	175	230	275	325	375	425
8	200	250	300	350	400	450
9	225	275	325	375	425	475

Where to Get Supplies

BLUE MOON FIBER ARTS

www.bluemoonfiberarts.com

THE FOLD

3316 Millstream Road
Marengo, IL
60152
U.S.A.

www.fibervilleusa.com/mall/thefold/welcome.html

DREAM IN COLOR YARNS

www.dreamincoloryarn.com

PURLESCENCE

586 S. Murphy Ave.
Sunnyvale, CA
94086
U.S.A.

www.purlescenceyarns.com

LETTUCE KNIT

70 Nassau St.
Toronto, ON
M5T 1M5
Canada

www.lettuceknit.com

LORNA'S LACES

www.lornaslaces.com

LOUET SALES

www.louet.com

KPIXIE

www.kpixie.com

THE YARN CO.

2274 Broadway @ 82nd St., 2nd Floor
New York, NY
10024
U.S.A.

www.theyarnco.com

KNITPICKS

www.knitpicks.com

Index

laddering, 47, 185, 192–193
large leg, 127
left-leaning cable (C4B), 40
left-leaning increase, 32–33
leg, 60. *See also individual patterns by name*
length, foot, 61
lifted increase, 32
light yarn weight, 5
locking marker, 18
locking ring marker, 27
Long-Tail Cast-On, 22–23
lower toe, 95, 103

M

M1 (Make 1) increase, 32–33
machine drying, 200
Machine Wash symbol, 196
machine washing, 199
machine-dyed yarn, 8
magic loop, 50–51, 167
magnetic board, 19
Make 1 (M1) increase, 32–33
material, 16–19, 208. *See also individual patterns by name; yarn*
mattress stitch, 96–98
medium yarn weight, 5
metal needle, 13
milk protein, 7
mistake. *See troubleshooting*

N

narrow toe, 76, 106
needle, 12–16, 40, 78–79, 96, 99. *See also type of needle by name*
needle check, 19
nonbinding edge, 133
non-slipped edge, 27
notions, 16–19
nylon, 6–7

P

p2tog (purl 2 together), 35
pattern, 10–11, 115. *See also individual patterns by name*

patterned sock, 74
pf&b (purl front and back), 31
picking up stitch, 26–29, 182–185
picking up wrap, 137, 146, 154, 162, 166, 171, 176
picot cuff, 163
picot edging, 130
plain stockinette stitch sock, 74
plastic needle, 13
protein fiber, 6
provisional cast-on, 24–25, 108
purl 2 together (p2tog), 35
purl bump, 184
purl front and back (pf&b), 31
purl stitch, 33, 184–187

R

reading chart, 38–39
recovering stitch, 73
repairing sock, 201–205
ribbing, 65, 129, 147–150. *See also types of ribbing by name*
right side of work, 191
right-leaning cable (C4F), 41
right-leaning increase, 32–33
row counter, 16
row gauge, 59

S

seam, flattening, 103
self-patterning yarn, 8
sewn bind-off method, 133
shoe size, 207
short-row heel, 68. *See also individual patterns by name*
short-row toe, 112–113
simple join, 52
size, 61, 207. *See also individual patterns by name*
skp (slip 1, knit 1, pass slipped stitch over), 37
slide-out, 12
slip, slip, knit (ssk), 36
slip 1, knit 1, pass slipped stitch over (skp), 37
slip-stitch color pattern, 11
slip-stitch heel pattern, 147
Slip-Stitch Ridges Socks, 140–143

Want instruction in other topics?

Check out these
All designed for visual learners—just like you!